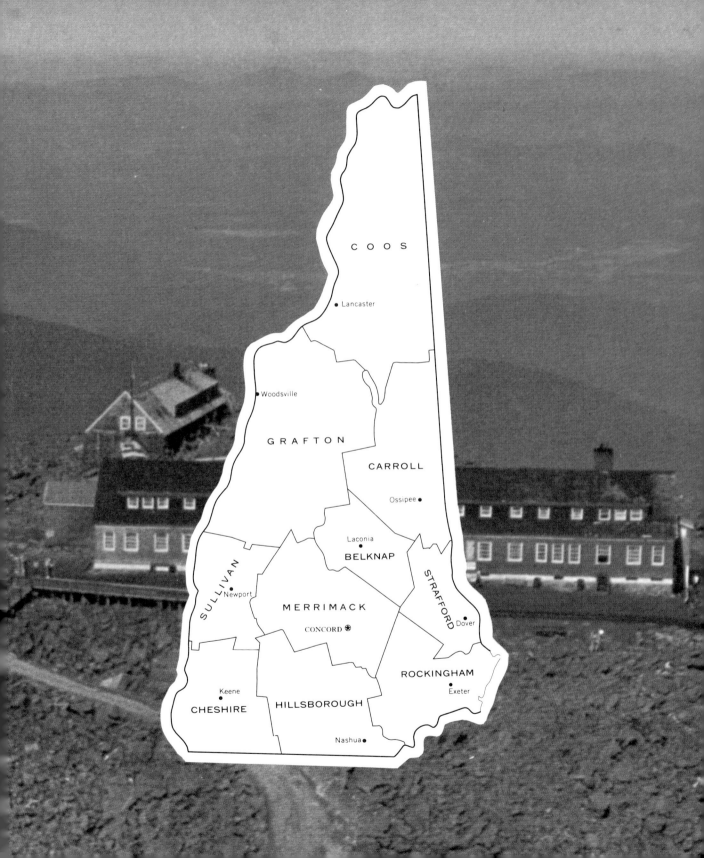

C O O S

● Lancaster

Woodsville ●

G R A F T O N

CARROLL

Ossipee ●

Laconia ●

BELKNAP

SULLIVAN

Newport ●

MERRIMACK

STRAFFORD

Dover ●

CONCORD ✸

ROCKINGHAM

Keene ●

CHESHIRE

HILLSBOROUGH

Exeter ●

Nashua ●

# The New
## Enchantment of America
# NEW HAMPSHIRE

By Allan Carpenter

 CHILDRENS PRESS, CHICAGO

# ACKNOWLEDGMENTS

**For assistance in the preparation of the revised edition, the author thanks:**
ANNE BRISSON, New Hampshire Department of Resources and Economic Development, ROBERT B. GRAHAM, JR., Director News Service, Dartmouth College, and DICK HAMILTON, White Mountain Attractions Association.

*American Airlines*—Anne Vitaliano, Director of Public Relations; *Capitol Historical Society,* Washington, D. C.; *Newberry Library,* Chicago, Dr. Lawrence Towner, Director; *Northwestern University Library,* Evanston, Illinois; *United Airlines*—John P. Grember, Manager of Special Promotions; Joseph P. Hopkins, Manager, News Bureau; Carl Provorse, *Carpenter Publishing House.*

UNITED STATES GOVERNMENT AGENCIES: *Department of Agriculture*—Robert Hailstock, Jr., Photography Division, Office of Communication; Donald C. Schuhart, Information Division, Soil Conservation Service. *Army*—Doran Topolosky, Public Affairs Office, Chief of Engineers, Corps of Engineers. *Department of Interior*—Louis Churchville, Director of Communications; EROS Space Program—Phillis Wiepking, Community Affairs; Charles Withington, Geologist; Mrs. Ruth Herbert, Information Specialist; Bureau of Reclamation; National Park Service—Fred Bell and the individual sites; Fish and Wildlife Service—Bob Hines, Public Affairs Office. *Library of Congress*—Dr. Alan Fern, Director of the Department of Research; Sara Wallace, Director of Publications; Dr. Walter W. Ristow, Chief, Geography and Map Division; Herbert Sandborn, Exhibits Officer. *National Archives*—Dr. James B. Rhoads, Archivist of the United States; Albert Meisel, Assistant Archivist for Educational Programs; David Eggenberger, Publications Director; Bill Leary, Still Picture Reference; James Moore, Audio-Visual Archives. *United States Postal Service*—Herb Harris, Stamps Division.

**For assistance in the preparation of the first edition, the author thanks:**
Consultant Lillian Bailey, author and teacher, Hanover High School; Paul E. Farnum, State Commissioner of Education; Division of Economic Development, State of New Hampshire; and Chamber of Commerce, Manchester.

**Illustrations on the preceeding pages:**

Cover photograph: Winter, near Peterborough, New Hampshire Department of Resources and Economic Development
Page 1: Commemorative stamps of historic interest
Pages 2-3: Summit of Mt. Washington, White Mountain Attractions Association, Inc., Dick Hamilton
Page 3: (Map) USDI Geological Survey
Pages 4-5: Northern New Hampshire, EROS Space Photo, USDI Geological Survey, EROS Data Center

Project Editor, Revised Edition:
  Joan Downing
Assistant Editor, Revised Edition:
  Mary Reidy

**Library of Congress Cataloging in Publication Data**

Carpenter, John Allan, 1917-
  New Hampshire.

  (His The new enchantment of America)
  SUMMARY: A presentation of the Granite State, including its history, resources, famous citizens, and places of interest to visit.
  1.  New Hampshire—Juvenile literature.  [1.  New Hampshire]
I.  Title.  II.  Series.
F34.3.C3  1979    974.2    79-11454
ISBN 0-516-04129-0

# Contents

The Old Man of the Mountain.

# A True Story to Set the Scene

## PLASTIC SURGERY FOR AN ELDERLY GENTLEMAN

"I am sorry to report, Governor, that the patient is slipping fast; immediate surgery is the only thing that will save him."

We do not have an actual record of what was said when the Reverend Guy Roberts and E. H. Geddes met with Governor Rolland Spaulding in August of 1915, but the above gives the general meaning of the report they made to the governor. The story of how the famous "patient" actually was saved by "surgery" that required a ton of special tools is one of the many stories of enchantment of New Hampshire.

Ever since it was discovered in the early 1800s, *The Old Man of the Mountain* had been one of America's most notable natural features. It is perched at the top of a cliff overlooking Franconia Notch.

"The face is made," according to Dr. Andrew H. McNair of Dartmouth College, "of several separate and independent ledges (of rock) so arranged along the cliff completely by chance, that when viewed from just the right angle they blend into each other to produce the face." There are five separate ledges; two make up the forehead, a jutting ledge forms the nose, a fourth the upper lip, and a fifth ledge provides the firm chin.

Many noted writers have described the Old Man, but none in more striking language than that of William Oakes: "His face is set and his countenance fixed and firm. He neither blinks at the near flashes of lightning nor flinches from the driving sleet and snow of the Franconia winter, which makes the very mercury of the thermometer shrink into its bulb and congeal."

There was great dismay in the 1880s when news was brought that the 30-ton (27-metric-ton) forehead stone was slipping. If it should slide from the head, it would probably break off the nose, and the magnificent profile would be ruined. Authorities who inspected the wonder said that nothing could be done.

One of the most ardent "supporters" of the Old Man was the Reverend Roberts. For years he tried to find someone who believed the natural treasure could be saved. Then in 1915 he met a stonecutting expert named Geddes. They went out to the profile, and their measurements showed that a slip of only 4 inches (101 millimeters) more would wreck the giant's features. However, Geddes said he was sure the Old Man could be saved.

They obtained the support of Governor Spaulding, and Geddes prepared three special sets of anchor irons up to 6 feet (1.8 meters) long and a full 2 inches (51 millimeters) in thickness. When he assembled all his necessary food and equipment, Geddes found he had a ton of gear, most of which he had to carry up the mountainside himself.

By this time it was almost October and the heights were cold. With his hands almost frozen, Geddes drilled holes in the granite, inserted his special anchors in exactly the right locations and drew them into position with mammoth turnbuckles. The "surgery" was completed in only eight days.

Twenty-two years later, at the age of seventy-one, E. H. Geddes once more climbed up to the brow of the Old Man and supervised the anchoring of one of the other stones. He found that the stone he had anchored so many years ago had slipped just 1/16 of an inch (1.6 millimeters).

One of New Hampshire's most important natural features had been preserved. The story forms a little epic that is quite typical of the determination, inventiveness, and courage of the people of New Hampshire, and calls attention to the countless natural wonders of the state.

# Lay of the Land

## WAUMBEK METHNA: THE WHITE MOUNTAINS

The aged Indian hunter had kept his coal burning during the bitter winter day in order to build his fire when he made his lonely camp for the night. When the flames started he watched with awe, for instead of a small campfire, a huge cloud of smoke and fire ascended. The earth rumbled and a vast pile of rocks began to rise up until they reached the very heavens themselves, still surrounded by a cloud of smoke. From this cloud a voice rumbled, saying "Here the Great Spirit will dwell, and watch over his favorite children."

This is only one of the many Indian legends concerning the formation of the White Mountains, which they called *Waumbek Methna,* "White Rock." Indians held this great mountain range in much respect as the true home of the Great Spirit.

Modern New Hampshire residents also respect the White Mountains, and they are considered the "backbone of New England." These rugged peaks are certainly the most important feature of the New Hampshire landscape. They cover an area of more than 1,200 square miles (3,108 square kilometers), and as someone so picturesquely remarked, "They lift their powdered wigs a mile into the air." Actually eight of the peaks are more than a mile (1.6 kilometers) high.

The most massive section of the New Hampshire mountains is the Presidential Range, with names of individual mountains honoring Presidents Jefferson, Adams, Madison, and Washington. Mount Washington, at 6,288 feet (1,917 meters), is the highest mountain not only in New Hampshire but in all of northeast America. Other important ranges are the Franconia and the Sandwich range.

Eight major passes, called notches in New Hampshire, slash across and through the state's ranges, making great gashes through which highways, railroads, and trails have been built. The most famous of these are Franconia Notch and Crawford Notch. Other notches are Kinsman, Pinkham, Bear, Carter, Jefferson, and Dixville.

The most southerly of the major mountains of the state is Grand

*Mount Chocorua*

Monadnock, only 3,165 feet (955 meters) tall but impressive because it stands alone and rises from more or less level surroundings. While staying at a resort on the side of Monadnock, Ralph Waldo Emerson wrote of his view from the mountain: "Every morn I lift my head,/See New England underspread/South from St. Lawrence to the Sound,/From Katskill east to the sea-bound."

## LAYOUT

Geographers divide New Hampshire into six major regions. The largest of these is the Connecticut Valley region, covering nearly a third of the total area of the state. Another river-based division is the Merrimack Valley. The Eastern Slope rises from the ocean front to reach the Merrimack Valley to the west and another division—the Lakes Region to the north. The White Mountain Region and the North Country, entirely within Coos County, complete the major geographical districts of New Hampshire.

Modern New Hampshire, which was named for the English County of Hampshire, is bounded by the neighboring states of Vermont, Massachusetts, and Maine. It has a short international boundary with the province of Quebec in Canada.

Seventeen and three-quarter miles (28.5 kilometers) of New Hampshire's borders make up the state's short but fascinatingly varied ocean shore. This encompasses Great Bay, described as being the most spacious tidewater bay in all of New England.

Off the coast are the Isles of Shoals. They were given this name because not far away are found enormous "shoals" or "schools" of fish. Four of these islands belong to New Hampshire. They are Lunging, Star, Seavey, and White.

## THE WATERS: FLOWING AND STANDING

Five river systems drain New Hampshire—the Merrimack, Piscataqua, Saco, Androscoggin, and Connecticut. The Connecticut, of course, is by far the largest of these. Although it forms the border between New Hampshire and Vermont, all of the Connecticut River up to the low-water mark on the west bank falls within the boundaries of New Hampshire.

The Indian name *Piscataqua* simply means "the river branches." For some distance the Piscataqua is an estuary, a kind of drowned valley; it adjoins Great Bay, another estuary.

The Ammonoosuc River has been called the "wildest stream in New England." Waters of this river fall 5,000 feet (1,524 meters) in its mad dash of only 30 miles (48 kilometers) to join the Connecticut River.

Altogether New Hampshire has the right to boast of 40,000 miles (64,374 kilometers) of picturesque rivers and streams.

Kona, an Indian warrior, loved Ellacaya, daughter of Chief Ahanton. Although Kona and Ahanton were enemies, Kona went to Ahanton and asked to marry his daughter. This bravery was admired so much by the chief that he permitted the marriage. Watching the happy couple paddle across the nearby large lake, Ahanton felt that the omens must be good, and he said, ''That all . . . may know of the peace between us, may these waters be called Winnipesaukee, the smile of the Great Spirit.'' This is only one of the many legends of how New Hampshire's largest lake was given its melodious sounding name. There are even more spellings of the name than legends— more than one hundred thirty. However, the state legislature made the present spelling official in 1931.

The shoreline of Winnipesaukee is one of the most irregular of all the country's large natural lakes. It is cut into by long peninsulas, which form bays that almost seem to be separate lakes. The lake's greatest length is 22 miles (35 kilometers) and its depth reaches 300 feet (91 meters). It is dotted with large numbers of islands. Long Island, the largest, extends for 3 miles (4.8 kilometers) and is 1 mile (1.6 kilometers) wide.

There are thirteen hundred ponds and lakes in New Hampshire, ranging in size from Winnipesaukee to such tiny dots as Profile Lake, nestled under the ''ear'' of The Old Man of the Mountain.

Other major New Hampshire lakes include Squam and Winnisquam, Sunapee, Newfound, Massabesic, Ossipee, Umbagog, shared with Maine, and Shadow Lake, made by damming the Connecticut River.


## IN ANCIENT AGES

Most of the state's lakes were formed by the action of the great glaciers which four times covered the state to enormous depths. Grinding relentlessly over the earth, they dug basins that filled with water to become lakes. Sometimes glacial till formed natural dams, which backed up water for miles.

Much of the form of New Hampshire was the doing of the glaciers. In addition to the lakes, huge circular valleys, known as glacial cirques, were scooped out. These form some of the most attractive scenery in the state. Southern New Hampshire has many hills shaped like whales' backs. These hills, sometimes clay and sometimes rock or other material, are called drumlins.

*Lighthouse at Ft. Point, New Castle.*

The glaciers were most "generous" to the state in the gift of boulders. They were trundled overland from their original sites with infinite slowness and "graciously" deposited in New Hampshire when the ice melted. These are found in the state in incredible numbers and sizes. Some areas are entirely covered with great glacial boulders in weird and jumbled masses.

It is hard to believe that the boulders, even on the lofty top of Mt. Washington, were deposited there by glaciers. The Madison boulder is said to be the largest "erratic" boulder in the United States. It weighs almost 8,000 tons (7,257 metric tons) and is over 80 feet (24 meters) long.

New Hampshire's famous flumes are also relics of the Ice Age, as are the Polar Caves near West Plymouth.

The weight of the glaciers was so tremendous that the level of the land was pressed down much lower than it now is. When the ice melted, the land began to rise slowly, like a sponge that expands when it is no longer being squeezed. The melting ice also raised the level of the seas, and parts of New Hampshire that had once been land were submerged. The famous Drowned Forest near Jenness Beach was probably growing on the New Hampshire shore until the sea rose to overwhelm it.

Many major features of New Hampshire were formed by forces much older than the glaciers. Fantastic slow upward and downward movements of the land raised mountain chains or brought in shallow seas. Much of the mountain region owes its present form to the centuries-old processes of erosion. The enormous quantities of granite that are such a marked feature of the state were forced to the surface by the unbelievable forces of heat and pressure deep in the earth.


## CLIMATE

Winters in New Hampshire are sometimes severe. The heavy snows help to pile up an average annual precipitation of as much as 45 inches (95 millimeters). Summers are so pleasant that countless numbers of prominent and wealthy people have selected the state above all others for their summer homes.

The influence of altitude on climate is shown by the fact that in going up Mt. Washington the temperature is lowered one degree (Fahrenheit) for every 300-foot (91-meter) increase in height. Some of the winter low temperatures and winds at the top of the mountain are among the most extreme known anywhere.

In fact, the mountain is known for its violent weather. The 231-mile-per-hour (372-kilometer-per-hour) wind recorded at the top of Mt. Washington in April, 1934, is a world wind record. The timberline on the mountain reflects the severe weather. On Washington the trees come to an end at an average height of 4,000 feet (1,219 meters), whereas the Rocky Mountain timberline averages about 10,000 feet (3,048 meters).

The growing season in New Hampshire ranges from 90 to 150 days.

# Footsteps on the Land

## THE ORIGINAL SETTLERS

Comparatively few relics showing a very old civilization have been found in New Hampshire. Howard Sargent of Hawthorne College excavated on the Connecticut and found what he believes to be evidences of prehistoric inhabitants of four thousand years ago. A stone weir built to keep the fish within a certain area near the outlet of Lake Winnipesaukee is one of the most interesting relics of prehistoric peoples in the state.

Early Europeans found the native inhabitants belonged to the Algonquin nation. The St. Francis Indians in what is now Canada laid claim to some regions of New Hampshire, although they probably never inhabited them permanently. They used the area as hunting and fishing preserves. Well-known names of the New Hampshire region included the Piscataqua, Coosuc, Ossipee, and Sokokis (or Pequawkets).

In 1627 the great Indian leader of the region, Passaconaway (Child of the Bear), united more than seventeen of the Indian groups of Central New England into the Penacook Confederacy. He took the title of first *Sagamon* or *Bashaba* and ruled wisely until his death in 1660. The Penacook Confederacy group that lived in New Hampshire were the Souhegan (or Nantacook), Nashua, Amoskeag, and Winnipesaukee. Other groups are often said to have been included, as well.

Passaconaway was a constant and good friend of the European settlers. As an old man he made a noted speech which has been reported in part: "The oak will soon break before the whirlwind... I commune with the Great Spirit. He whispers me now—'Tell your people, Peace, Peace, is the only hope of your race. I have given fire and thunder to the pale faces for weapons—I have made them plentier than the leaves of the forest and still shall they increase! These meadows they shall turn with the plow—these forests shall fall by the axe—the pale faces shall live upon your hunting grounds, and make their villages upon your fishing places!'

American Indian Kings, *anonymous after John Verelst, 1716, a mural at Warner House, Portsmouth.*

"The Great Spirit says this, and it must be so! We are few and powerless before them! We must bend before the storm! The wind blows hard! The old oak trembles! Its branches are gone! Its sap is frozen! It bends! It falls! Peace, Peace . . . is the command of the Great Spirit—and the wish—the last wish of Passaconaway." Few seers have been more accurate prophets.

So great was the reputation of Passaconaway that he impressed even Europeans. One of them wrote that the Indian leader was able to "make the water burne, the rocks move, the trees dance, metamorphise himself into a flaming man. . ."

Upon his death, the Indian legend says, Passaconaway was carried into the heights of Mount Washington on a sledge hauled by a fierce team of snarling wolves.

The Indians of the New Hampshire region grew corn as their principal crop; pumpkins, beans, and squash were also staples. Even tobacco was grown regularly and much enjoyed. They pounded their corn in mortars, sometimes using the potholes hollowed by nature into the rocks. This pounded corn was hominy. The Indians taught

18

European settlers how to cut a ring of bark from the trees to girdle them. When the trees died, sunlight reached the ground, and crops could be grown even before the trees were cleared away.

The Indians made their tools and weapons at several quarries found around the state, such as the quarry workshop at Newfound Lake. One of their favorite materials for arrowheads and spear points was the beautiful jasper found at Jasper Cave near Berlin.

Many Indian legends are favorites even today.

One of these was the legend of Chocorua, a Pequawket leader; he was said to have left his son to stay with Europeans while he went away on a journey. The son was accidentally poisoned. For vengeance Chocorua killed all the members of the family, and later was killed himself on the slopes of the mountain that was given his name—Mt. Chocorua. Before he died he pronounced a curse on any Europeans who would live in the region. For years cattle sickened and died in the region and it was considered the result of the curse until a deadly natural chemical was found in the water.

A well-known painting by Thomas Cole, *The Death of Chocorua,* was based on this legend.

The strongest link with the Indians is the many names of places in the state—names like Sunapee, Baboosic, and Massabesic lakes—the Piscataquog and Soucook rivers, and such towns as Contoocook, Penacook, Suncook, and many others.


## BEGINNINGS

There seems little doubt that Norse explorers were sailing along the coast of New England by the year 1000 A.D. It is probable that they at least made landings and explorations in New Hampshire, but no reliable records of this have been uncovered. Carvings on a boulder found near Hampton are considered by some experts as proof that Norse explorers were in that region around the year 1100, but no one is certain of such relics.

Giovanni de Verrazano probably sighted the White Mountains from the sea in 1508, but almost a hundred years passed before the first recorded visit of Europeans to New Hampshire. Martin Pring, in 1603, ventured up the Piscataqua River in his vessels the *Discoverer* and *Speedwell* in a search for sassafras, valued in Europe as a flavorful type of tea and as a flavoring for beers.

Explorer-colonizer Samuel de Champlain pushed up the Piscataqua River in 1605. It is thought that he landed where the community of Rye is now located. The great mountain far inland that he sighted on this journey was probably Mt. Washington.

In 1614 Captain John Smith, who had left his post in the Virginia Colony several years before, explored the New England seacoast quite thoroughly, including New Hampshire. His report greatly encouraged a number of English people to make new plans to colonize this area. When Prince Charles of England read Smith's report, the prince called the area New England, a name the region has had ever since.

Captain Smith, Captain John Mason, and others formed a group known as the Plymouth Company, later the Council of New England, and King James I of England granted a charter that gave the council a vast tract in the New World. The council then parceled out smaller grants to various people. Sir Ferdinando Gorges and John Mason received the right to a large tract that included all of present-day New Hampshire east of the Merrimack River, as well as a large part of present-day Maine.

In 1623 David Thomson, along with a few colonists whom he brought, made a settlement in the town of Rye, originally part of Portsmouth. This is usually considered the first European settlement in New Hampshire. A few months later, Edward Hilton and some others settled at Hilton's Point, now Dover, about 6 miles (9.6 kilometers) up the Piscataqua River.

David Thomson left in 1626; representatives of John Mason took over a hillside thick with wild strawberries, and the new settlement was called Strawbery Banke. This, of course, later became Portsmouth (in 1653).

Mason and Gorges divided their holdings in 1629, and Mason took an area that he called New Hampshire, giving the region that name for the first time.

*Giovanni de Verrazano*

In 1637 the Reverend John Wheelwright made his way through the wilderness from Boston, where he had political and religious differences with the Puritans. Wheelwright had an interesting and forceful personality. At Cambridge University in England he was a classmate of Oliver Cromwell, later the lord protector of England, who said he respected Wheelwright in a football game more than any other opponent.

In 1638, Wheelwright received a deed for land from the *Sagamore* (chief) of the Squamscott tribe, whose name was Wehanownowitt. With a few settlers who also held his religious views, Wheelwright established the settlement of Exeter, the third in New Hampshire.

Also in 1638 Hampton was settled by a group from Massachusetts who recognized the authority of Massachusetts in the area.

These were the four original settlements of New Hampshire—Dover, Portsmouth, Exeter, and Hampton. The many grants of land made by different authorities had overlapping boundaries, and there were numerous conflicting claims. As time went on, Massachusetts claimed more and more of the region, and by 1642 the four New Hampshire towns submitted to the government of the Massachusetts Bay Colony. However, each New Hampshire town was permitted to send its own deputy as its representative in the Massachusetts general court.

It is interesting to note that life was very democratic in the New Hampshire towns of this period. All questions were discussed and debated in open meetings and decided by the voters. A representative of the king reported that "the lowest mechanics discussed the most important points of government with the utmost freedom."

For a considerable period, settlement did not expand much beyond the original four towns. Most of the settlers came to the area for the economic opportunities to be found there, rather than for religious reasons, as in Massachusetts. The main business activities of the early period were fur trading, lumbering, fishing, and some shipbuilding. Flour mills had been built as early as 1630, taking advantage of the power in New Hampshire's rushing streams.

## THE LONG WARPATH

For more than fifty years, the settlers remained on good terms with the Indians. But many Indian leaders began to see that as more and more Europeans came in, the Indians' homes and lives were in danger. The Indian leader known as King Philip stirred up the warriors, and soon almost all the English colonies in America were drawn into what was known as King Philip's War. For almost a hundred years New Hampshire suffered almost constant terror from the Indians.

In 1675 Durham experienced the first attack of King Philip's War, and fierce raids were made again and again at Durham and elsewhere. At last King Philip and his allies were defeated, but it was not long until in 1689 England and France went to war. From 1689 to 1763 the two nations fought four major wars, and in between these there was an almost uninterrupted clash between the English and French colonists of the New World. Both sides encouraged their Indian allies to fight the "enemy," and the French were particularly relentless in this. Many frightful raids in New Hampshire were led by

22

*Indians attack a settlement.*

French military officers with picked crews of soldiers along with many Indian braves.

The British, in their turn, offered high rewards for anyone bringing in an Indian scalp, and some were not particular about whether the scalp had belonged to a friendly Indian or a foe.

In 1689 a French-Indian war party swooped down on Dover and almost completely destroyed it. Those who were not killed were taken captive to Canada, and only a few were ever lucky enough to return to their homes.

From this time on, no colonist in New Hampshire was ever sure at what minute he might be called on to defend his home and his life and his loved ones.

The historian Belknap described a typical massacre, the attack on Durham in 1694: "The defenseless houses were nearly all set on fire, the inhabitants being either killed or taken in them, or else in endeavoring to fly to the garrisons. Some escaped by hiding in the bushes and other secret places." With more than a hundred killed, this was probably the worst attack in New Hampshire of the series of Indian wars.

Charlestown was the frontier of settlement for many years, and in this advanced and exposed position it suffered particularly from the French and Indian attacks.

The records are filled with tales of escape and bravery in New

Hampshire. The most famous of these was the exploit of Hannah Dustin near Concord.

On March 15, 1697, only a week after her child had been born, Indians captured forty-year-old Mrs. Dustin at her home in Haverhill, Massachusetts. Cotton Mather wrote a well-known account of her experiences: "... Dustin and her nurse notwithstanding her present condition travelled... one hundred and fifty miles (241 kilometers) within a few days ensuing, without any sensible damage to her health. ... But on April 30 (It was really March 30) while they were yet, it may be, an hundred and fifty miles (241 kilometers) from the Indian town, a little before break of day, when the whole crew was in a dead sleep, (Reader, see if it prove not so,) one of these women took up a resolution to imitate the action of Jael upon Sisera; and being where she had not her own life secured unto her, she thought she was not forbidden by any law to take away the life of the murderers by whom her child had been butchered.

"She hardened the nurse and the youth to assist her in this enterprise; and all furnishing themselves with hatchets for this purpose, they struck such home-blows upon the heads of their oppressors, that ere they could any of them struggle into effectual resistance, at the feet of these poor prisoners they bowed, they fell, they lay down; at their feet they bowed, they fell where they bowed, there they fell down dead. The two women and the youth then followed the Merrimack back to Haverhill, carrying 10 scalps, for which they received a bounty of fifty pounds." Mather does not tell how they drifted down the Merrimack River for forty miles (64 kilometers) in an Indian canoe until they found refuge at the home of John Lovewell, Sr., at Nashua.

A Hannah Dustin monument stands today near Concord where she and her fellow prisoners rose up and gained their freedom.

Another one of the occasional personal triumphs against the Indians was that of Jabez Dame of Somersworth. Seeing Indians coming, he hid beneath the boards of his roof. When they found no one at the house they set it afire. After they left, Jabez crawled down, set another fire in the yard so that the Indians would continue to see smoke, then put out the fire in his house.

One of the more intense periods of warfare is known as Captain Lovewell's War—1722-25. After a successful expedition against the Indians, Captain John Lovewell was ambushed while he and his men were saying their prayers. Both Captain Lovewell and Chief Paugus who led the Indians were killed in this struggle, and only fourteen of Lovewell's forty-six men reached safety.

Among the most heroic defenses of the Indian wars was that of the John Kilburn family of Walpole, in 1755. For hours, Kilburn, his son, wife, daughter, and two other men held off an attack by one-hundred-seventy Indians. When the Kilburns grew low on bullets they used a blanket to deflect enemy shot coming through their roof, melted them down and cast new bullets, which they fired back at the attackers. The Indians finally gave up, buried their dead, including their leader Chief Philip, and left the scene.

Naturally there were few humorous sides to these brutal wars, but the request of Major John Gilman might be put in that category. Major Gilman escaped the massacre of Fort William and Mary in 1757. He later filed a claim with the government with an "Inventory of cloaths &c, Taken by the Indian." His list of losses included a wig, waistcoats, gold-laced hats, coats, a two-volume Bible, and an ivory book. Some fighters came equipped for almost everything, it would seem, according to this list. For these and other losses the government reimbursed him three hundred pounds.

The source of most of the Indian raids in New Hampshire was the St. Francis group's village of St. Francis in Canada. In October, 1759, Major Robert Rogers led a daring and noted raid on the St. Francis village, and almost wiped out this enemy headquarters. Pursued by Indian allies of the St. Francis, and cut off from the way they had come, the Rangers made one of history's most heroic retreats. They separated into small groups and made their way down the Connecticut Valley, suffering incredible hardships. Although almost starved, most of the groups made their way back.

The last great war of this series was known in America as the French and Indian War. When it drew to a close after the fall of French Canada in 1759, most of the Indian troubles in New Hampshire were over.

*Bretton Woods with the Mt. Washington
Hotel in the background, site of the 1944
International Monetary Conference.*

# Yesterday and Today

## UNDER ROYAL GOVERNORS

Although the Indian wars greatly hampered progress, much had been going on. New Hampshire had separated from Massachusetts in 1679 and was made a royal colony. Unlike most of the other colonies, the king did not give New Hampshire a charter. The colony was governed by a president and council, appointed by the crown; there was a lower house elected by the people. New Hampshire was part of the Dominion of New England from 1686 to 1689, then rejoined Massachusetts briefly in 1689. By 1692 New Hampshire was again a separate governing unit, even though from 1699 to 1741 New Hampshire and Massachusetts shared the same royal governor.

In 1741 Benning Wentworth was appointed royal governor of New Hampshire, alone. He was followed in 1767 by his nephew, John Wentworth, the last royal governor.

Benning Wentworth claimed for New Hampshire all of Vermont, although this was disputed by New York. He gave out liberal grants of land in Vermont, in spite of all protests. Whenever the Wentworths chartered land, they always found a clever manner of reserving a choice portion of it for their own personal estates. Benning Wentworth governed in an almost regal manner from his splendid residence in Little Harbor.

Meanwhile, New Hampshire was growing; by 1732, thirty-eight towns had received their charters. Jeremy Belknap wrote an interesting description of business conditions in New Hampshire in 1737: "The trade of the province at this time consisted chiefly in the exports of lumber and fish to Spain and Portugal and the Caribee Islands. The mast trade was wholly confined to Great Britain. In the winter small vessels went to the southern colonies with English and West Indian goods and returned with corn and pork. The manufacture of iron within the province lay under discouragement and want of experienced and industrious workmen. Woolen manufacture was diminished and sheep were scarcer than formerly, the common land on which they used to feed being fenced in by the proprietors. The manufacture of linen was much increased by means of the emigrants from Ireland who were skilled in that business. No improvements were made in agriculture...."

The present boundary with Massachusetts had been established in 1740, but New Hampshire continued to hope that Vermont would remain part of New Hampshire. These dreams were shattered in 1764 when the king established the western boundary of New Hampshire along the west bank of the Connecticut River, where it has remained ever since.

An interesting sidelight of the period of the 1760s and '70s is the fact that large numbers of public improvements were accomplished through lotteries, which were extremely popular.


## PRELUDE TO REVOLUTION

During this period, from Maine to Georgia the people of the British colonies were growing increasingly unhappy about the rule of the mother country. The "taxes without representation," the high-handed manner of the London government, and the abuses of royal officials in the colonies were among the leading causes of discontent.

In New Hampshire one of the main reasons for dissatisfaction concerned the "broad-arrow" trees. The tallest, straightest, finest trees were marked by the king's representative with a slash on the bark in the shape of an arrow. These trees were reserved for masts in his majesty's navy. There was severe punishment for those who cut a broad-arrow tree in defiance of the law. As early as 1734 there had been a mast tree riot at Exeter.

The fact that the royal governors, the Wentworths, had reserved for themselves more than 100,000 acres (40,469 hectares) of the finest land in New Hampshire could hardly have made the people feel more kindly toward the king's government.

There was an armed revolt in December, 1774. On December 13 Paul Revere galloped to Portsmouth, in one of his many "rides," bearing the news that no more supplies of gunpowder or items of war were to be shipped to the colonies. The next day an "army" of about four hundred men calling themselves the Portsmouth Sons of Liberty and the Patriots from New Castle, under John Sullivan, captured the supplies of gunpowder at Fort Constitution (then called Fort William and Mary) near New Castle. They hid the powder under the pulpit of the Durham meeting house.

Six months later, in June, 1775, Governor John Wentworth fled from the colony, and a Committee of Safety was set up to provide a temporary government. The capital was taken from Portsmouth to Exeter, because there were too many Tories (British supporters) in Portsmouth. On January 5, 1776, a provisional constitution was adopted. This was the first adopted by any of the colonies; it provided a house of representatives and a council, with Meshech Weare as first councilor and chairman of the Committee of Safety.

The new government voted for independence from Great Britain on June 15, 1776.


## FUEL FOR THE FLAMES OF REVOLT

New Hampshire was the only one of the original thirteen colonies in which no actual battles of the Revolutionary War were fought. However, the people and resources of the state played an important part in that conflict.

Governor John Wentworth had been proud of his militia, keeping them well drilled and equipped. As soon as word of the battles of Lexington and Concord reached the militia, the boys took the governor's uniforms and marched off to war, forming three of the best-organized and equipped regiments of the Revolution.

In preparation for the conflict he foresaw, Dr. Henry Dearborn had been drilling a group of about a hundred men. On April 20, 1775, when news of Lexington and Concord reached them, they assembled, and at 4:00 P.M., under Dr. Dearborn's command, set off for Medford, Massachusetts, a distance of 60 miles (96.5 kilometers). Tradition says they reached there at 4:00 A.M., probably the longest and fastest night military march on record.

New Hampshire men played a large part in the Battle of Bunker

Hill, and it is probable the results might have been much different without the powder that the Portsmouth Sons of Liberty had seized at Fort William and Mary and brought in for the battle.

The familiar phrase "Don't fire till you see the whites of their eyes," supposed to have been used at Bunker Hill, had a peculiar meaning for one New Hampshire man. Because of the shortage of ammunition, the Americans at the Battle of Bunker Hill were given strict instructions not to fire until the order was heard. As the British troops came closer and closer, the tension grew until Major John Simpson of Deerfield Parade could stand it no longer and fired without orders. The next day he was court-martialed for his disobedience, but was let off with a reprimand. He went on to serve with honor.

The First New Hampshire Regiment saw eight years and eight months of service in the Revolutionary War. This is thought to be the longest record of service of any regiment in that war.

Navy leader John Paul Jones made his headquarters at Portsmouth so that he could supervise the building of his noted ship, the *Ranger*. More than a hundred ships out of Portsmouth operated as privateers, harassing British shipping and capturing supplies during the war.

Dr. Ezra Green of Dover served under Captain Jones on the *Ranger,* and in his diary the doctor recorded one of the nation's historic moments: "Saturday, 14th feb'y (1778)... Came to sail at 4 o'clock P.M. saluted the french Admiral & rec'd nine guns in return *this is the first salute ever pay'd the American flagg."*

Exeter was considered the heart of New Hampshire's wartime support during the Revolution. There was said to be but a single Tory in Exeter. This was the town printer, who was seized for counterfeiting the local currency to help the British.


## THE DECIDING STATE

A strange event occurred in 1778 when thirty-five towns of New Hampshire attempted to join the independent Republic of Vermont.

However, the union never received official recognition, and it did not last long.

The end of the Revolution left New Hampshire with mountainous war debts. Efforts to overcome this by printing more and more paper money were not effective. A new state constitution was adopted in 1784.

By a vote of 57 to 46, New Hampshire became the ninth state to vote for ratification of the federal Constitution—June 21, 1788. Since nine states were required to make the new Constitution the official government of the country, New Hampshire was the deciding state in putting the United States into actual operation.

The new state was honored in 1789 by a visit from President George Washington. The distinguished visitor was rowed about the harbor of Portsmouth in state "in a great red, white, and blue barge, amid the acclamations of hundreds on the shore." Along with his hosts, Washington let down a line to do some fishing but caught only one, weighing about half a pound (.2 kilogram).

One day in 1805 Luke Brooks and Francis Whitcomb were surveying a road in Franconia Notch. They knelt down by the waters of a lake to splash cool water on their faces, and when they looked up they saw, apparently carved out of the mountain itself, a great human head, far in the distance. This is considered to be the first sighting by any European of New Hampshire's most famous landmark, *The Old Man of the Mountain*.

The capital of New Hampshire was moved permanently in 1808 from Portsmouth to Concord.

When the new United States and England again went to war in 1812, New Hampshire was again one of the best prepared. The state militia counted three divisions of six brigades and thirty-seven regiments. Governor John Langdon was able to call thirty-five thousand New Hampshire men to service through the draft. Once again New Hampshire privateers, numbering about fourteen, preyed on English shipping.

One of the country's most famous cases of law came about when the state, in a dispute with Dartmouth College, attempted to take over the management of this private institution. When the case came

*A portrait of Daniel Webster.*

before the United States Supreme Court, Daniel Webster, the most celebrated graduate of Dartmouth, pleaded the cause of the college and won his case in a decision handed down by Chief Justice John Marshall in 1819. Webster had made a statement to the court, which later became very famous: "It is a small college, gentlemen, but there are those who love it."

The case was particularly important because it protected the rights of private property and its management.

An interesting and revealing account of life in New Hampshire during this period was given in 1821 in the New Hampshire *Patriot:* "Farmers hired their help for nine or ten dollars a month—some clothing and the rest cash. Carpenters' wages, one dollar a day; journeyman carpenters, fifteen dollars a month; and apprentices to serve six to seven years, had ten dollars the first year, twenty the second, and so on and to clothe themselves.

"Breakfast generally consisted of potatoes roasted in the ashes, a 'bannock' made of meal and water and baked on a maple chip set before the fire. Pork was plenty. If 'hash' was had for breakfast, all ate from the platter, without plates or table-spread. Apprentices and farm boys had for supper a bowl of scalded milk and a brown crust, or bean porridge, or 'pop-robbin.' There was no such thing as tumblers, nor were they asked if they would have tea or coffee."

For nearly sixty years no one was quite sure where New Hampshire stopped and Canada began. The Treaty of Paris that ended the Revolutionary War was quite vague, because no one was familiar with the district and there were no surveys. A number of settlers in the northernmost part of New Hampshire had illegally bought land from the Indians, but New Hampshire refused to recognize these; Canada also laid claim to the territory.

At last in 1832 the three hundred or more settlers of the region declared themselves independent and created the Indian Stream Republic, which they considered a separate nation. However, they met with many difficulties and the people were divided. Both Canada and the United States continued to press their claims. At last the governor of New Hampshire sent militiamen to keep the Indian Stream Republic in line. Finally, the Webster-Ashburton Treaty of 1840 set the boundaries at their present limits, and the Indian Stream Republic was absorbed into New Hampshire.

The state's only native-born president, Franklin Pierce, became in 1852 the fourteenth man elected to that high office. In that same year the first Summit House was built on the lofty top of Mt. Washington; it was constructed of lumber and other material laboriously brought up the slopes by pack horses.


## THE CIVIL WAR

Slavery had never had much of a place in New Hampshire. Most of the people, who prized individual freedom, strongly opposed slavery. In 1835 John Dickson of Keene was the first congressman who ever dared to rise and make a speech against slavery in the Congress of the United States.

Because of its location on the Canadian border, the state was in a strategic position to help runaway slaves escape over the "Underground Railroad." The Carleton House in Littleton was one of the important "stations" on the Underground Railroad.

When war came, New Hampshire maintained its reputation for readiness by sending the first completely equipped regiment to arrive at the front from any state. The First New Hampshire Regiment had full equipment of uniforms, ammunition and arms, supply and hospital wagons, baggage, and other necessities.

As the war drew to a close and Richmond surrendered, the Thirteenth Regiment of New Hampshire was privileged to lead the Union forces into that long-sought goal of the war.

Army and navy service called 32,500 men from New Hampshire during the Civil War. About 6,500 from the state served in other ways during the war and 4,685 died.


## A MODERN STATE

Sylvester Marsh's first little picturesque cog engine puffed, chugged, and wheezed its way to the top of Mt. Washington in 1869. In that same year another chugging and wheezing vehicle was invented by Enos M. Clough of Sunapee. After fourteen years of trying, he made a successful horseless carriage propelled by a two-cylinder engine. With 5,463 parts, three forward speeds and three reverse, it was much in advance of its time. However, the city fathers made Clough give it up because it made too much noise, and the fame he may have deserved never came to Enos Clough.

The first party of scientists ever to spend the winter on the top of Mt. Washington began their vigil in November of 1870. Their thrilling reports of weather phenomena surprised even residents of nearby villages.

*Daniel Webster's birthplace.*

During the period of 1873 to 1897, six New Hampshire towns qualified as cities and were incorporated. These were Keene (1873), Rochester (1891), Somersworth and Laconia (1893), Franklin (1895), and Berlin (1897).

Just before the turn of the century, in 1899, the motorized age was ushered into the state when the first automobile wheezed its way to the top of Mt. Washington. F.O. Stanley was the driver in his Stanley Steamer.

World attention turned to the Portsmouth area in 1905 when representatives of Russia and Japan met there at the invitation of President Theodore Roosevelt. The bitter Russo-Japanese War was brought to a close with the signing of the Treaty of Portsmouth on September 5.

That same year, in one of the most spectacular fires ever seen, the Summit House on the top of Mt. Washington was destroyed. The blaze could be seen for miles.

When the United States entered World War I in 1917, the first of a total of more than 20,000 persons from the state began their service. Of these, 697 died.

The king of England had placed the western boundary of New Hampshire at the west bank of the Connecticut River in 1764, but the matter was not finally settled until the Supreme Court of the United States reaffirmed this line as the boundary in 1934. This gave New Hampshire sole control of many valuable water rights, but it also made the state solely responsible for financing bridges and other improvements.

During 1927 and 1936 New Hampshire suffered from some of the most extensive floods in the state's history.

In World War II over 60,000 New Hampshire men and women were in the service of their country. Of these, 1,599 died.

Much of the advancement and improvement in the state during this period came about through developments in agriculture, manufacturing, mining, transportation, communication, and education.

In New Hampshire's early days, many of the public improvements were financed by lotteries. Private individuals also often offered a lottery prize and sold tickets to pay for some pet project or necessity. New Hampshire was following long-established historical precedent when in 1964 the state ran the first legal sweepstakes lottery in the United States since 1894.

In 1974-75, the entire nation watched the strange disputed U.S. Senate election between Republican L.C. Wyman and Democrat J.A. Durkin. When the Senate ordered a new election in 1975, Durkin won. In 1976 another boundary dispute was settled by the U.S. Supreme Court. The court awarded most of the disputed coastal waters to Maine.

During the 1970s New Hampshire experienced almost unprecedented industrial growth, especially in the southern region. The absence of general state sales and income taxes has proved extremely attractive. Tourist attractions also bring in about half a billion dollars a year.

## THE PEOPLE AND THEIR BELIEFS

People from more than fifty nations have settled in New Hampshire. However, over half of all the people from outside the United States are from one country—Canada. Only 5 percent of those from Canada are not French-Canadian. The French-Canadian people have maintained many of their own traditions and culture and have supported French parochial schools. French-Canadian groups are especially important in the cities. Manchester is more than a third French-Canadian.

Only 361 Indians remained in New Hampshire, according to the 1970 census; there were only 3,000 blacks, 360 Japanese, and 420 Chinese.

In matters of religion, the people of early New Hampshire were much more tolerant than their neighbors in Massachusetts. Only the Quakers were persecuted. Quakers Marmaduke Stevenson and William Robinson were banished, and when they returned without permission they were hanged, in 1659. Three years later at Dover three Quaker women who had tried to preach there were made to bare their backs in the middle of winter and were whipped out of town. However, it was not long before Quakers were welcomed in New Hampshire where they made their homes in peace.

The records show that only one woman ever was accused of witchcraft in New Hampshire, although in the neighboring colonies "witches" were being punished and even being put to death. When Goody Walford of Portsmouth was accused of being a witch, she sued the accusers for scandal and won a judgment for damages against them.

Apparently the first church in New Hampshire was organized in 1638 at Hampton. The first Episcopal chapel was founded also in 1638, at Portsmouth. The first Roman Catholic church was not founded in New Hampshire until 1823, at Claremont.

*A typical scene of a covered bridge and church in New Hampshire.*

Until 1819 the Congregational Church was the state church of New Hampshire and received support from the state. After that year, the people were no longer taxed to support a church. Until 1876 the state constitution required all United States congressmen and senators from New Hampshire, as well as the governor, to "be of the Protestant religion."

New Hampshire was notable for keeping its ministers in one place. Joseph Adams served as the minister at Newington for sixty-eight years. In two hundred twenty-five years, only nine ministers served the South Parish Church of Portsmouth.

This perhaps is indicative of the sturdiness of health and character for which the people of New Hampshire have so long been noted. As one supporter of the state put it, "I have never been quite able to define it, but there is something in the very air that seems to be building the unique character that is our most important product."

38

# Natural Treasures

## FORESTS AND FLOWERS

The most important single natural resource on New Hampshire is the handsome forest cover that spreads over 84 percent of the land area of the state, encompassing a total of about 5,000,000 acres (2,023,430 hectares). Of this, 678,000 acres (274,387 hectares) are protected by a part of the White Mountain National Forest.

Silver, red, sugar, and mountain maples blanket the state with a burst of color in the fall. Birch, beech, oak, hickory, and butternut are other common hardwoods. Spruce in the north and white pine in the south are the principal evergreens. Hemlock, balsam, arbovitae, and juniper also are found.

There is an abundance of low-lying shrubs. Many people are surprised to find mountain laurel and rhododendron this far north, let alone the fact that there is a Rhododendron State Park. The host of wild flowers includes several members of the orchid family, such as lady slippers; trailing arbutus, trillium, honeysuckle, and parasitic Indian pipe are among other interesting flowers.

Among the state's floral delights are the Alpine gardens found in the high places. Above the timberline in the Presidential Range is a true Alpine zone that is unique in eastern United States. Here are the low growing, fragile appearing flowers, shrubs, and mosses that usually are found only in Arctic regions.

## WILDLIFE

Some kinds of big game, such as deer, are still plentiful, but others have disappeared or are scarce. A large number of moose once roamed the state.

Buffalo once were numerous, and when these animals began to vanish, one of the first steps ever taken to preserve big game was organized in New Hampshire. This was the formation of the American Bison Society at Croydon Flat.

*Autumn in New Hampshire.*

One of the earliest projects to preserve wildlife began at Croydon Flat under the inspiration of Austin Corbin, who bought land and purchased game to be protected in the Corbin Game Preserve. Buffalo there were some of the largest in the country.

Bear, wildcat, wild boar, and smaller animals are still available to the hunter in New Hampshire.

Ruffed grouse, waterfowl, woodcock, and pheasants are among the most popular game birds in the state. John Josselyn in 1672 spotted in the "high hills of Ossapy a pihannaw, or mechquan, much like the description of the Indian ruck (roc), a monstrous great bird." Much to their disappointment, other bird lovers have never spotted a monster Indian roc in New Hampshire. This was the legendary bird that was supposed to have carried off Sinbad the Sailor. However, almost three hundred other species of birds have been observed in New Hampshire.

Nearly a hundred kinds of fish are found in the rivers, lakes, and ponds. Among the most popular with fishermen are brook, golden, and lake trout, bass, landlocked salmon, pickerel, horned pout, pike, and whitefish. Winter fishing is popular for pickerel, perch, lake trout, and whitefish, and the frozen surfaces of lakes are dotted with "bob houses." Also popular is ice fishing on Great Bay.

New Hampshire's short seacoast offers some surprising salt-water fishing for such favorites as cod, flounder, mackerel, smelt, bluefin tuna, pollock, and striped bass.

## MINERALS

Minerals of New Hampshire that have a commercial value include fluorite, feldspar, mica, garnet, some copper, and, of course, granite, which provides the nickname "The Granite State."

Rock hounds and collectors could find more than two hundred minerals in New Hampshire to add to their collections, including aquamarine (beryl), topaz, amethyst, and other semiprecious stones. Specimens of radioactive and fluorescent minerals are fairly common in several localities.

*Right: Many old skills, such as metalsmithing, are still cherished. Below: Collecting maple syrup.*

# People Use Their Treasures

## MANUFACTURING, MINING, FARMING

Manufacturing in New Hampshire began as early as 1631, when the first mills were set up to grind grain and saw timber. The state's first paper mill was begun in 1793. In 1634 some of the iron ore of the colony was shipped to England. Iron ore found at Ore Hill in 1805 at one time was the richest known in the country, but it was superseded by richer finds in other states, and little use is now made of the state's iron ores.

Shipbuilding also began early in Piscataqua Bay. It is important to New Hampshire today, since the Portsmouth area profits from the jobs and commerce of the United States Naval Yard and other ship-building activities, most of which are just across the state line at Kittery, Maine.

One of the most interesting manufacturing operations in our history developed in New Hampshire. Lewis Downing began to manufacture wagons in his plant at Concord in 1813. He started with capital of only sixty dollars. In 1826 Stephen Abbott joined the firm that soon became Abbott and Downing Company, and they began to make stagecoaches. Throughout the development of the entire American West, the Concord Stagecoach made by Abbott and Downing was known to everyone. Although the automobile has made it extinct, the Concord coach still lives in a thousand television and movie episodes and in the hearts of those who consider it a symbol of the "romance" of the frontier.

Changing times and customs also spelled the end of the leadership of another New Hampshire company. At one time the Kilburn Factory at Littleton was the greatest manufacturer of stereoscopes anywhere.

Another New Hampshire pioneering manufacturing effort was the successful building of the first watches ever made by machinery, at the Nashua Watch Factory. Still another notable Nashua firm is the Nashua Manufacturing Company, generally considered to be the largest blanket mill in the world.

An even larger textile house was the vast Amoskeag Manufacturing Company, at one time the world's largest cotton mills. However, the huge operation failed to keep up with modern trends and was forced into bankruptcy in 1935.

Maple products date from before European settlement in New Hampshire. The most recent count of maple producers in the state was over two hundred. At most maple-sugar houses, visitors may enjoy a sugaring-off party during the short sap season, usually from February 28 to April 10. At these parties the attraction is syrup on snow, commonly called "leather aprons," with sour pickles (of all things!), unsweetened doughnuts, and hot coffee.

Many traditional handmade products of New Hampshire, such as hand-wrought iron ware from the master blacksmith's shop, have been dying out. The League of New Hampshire Arts and Crafts does everything it can to encourage skilled handworkers. One of its projects is the League of New Hampshire Craftsmen's Fair held annually in early August at Newbury.

Present-day manufacturing in New Hampshire is modern and up-to-date, with many of the giant companies having branches in the state. New industry is rapidly developing in New Hampshire, including such massive operations as the Bailey Company of Seabrook, world's largest producer of molded shapes.

The current value of manufactured products of New Hampshire totals more than one and a half billion dollars annually. New Hampshire is rated as the nation's "second-most industrialized state in proportion to population."

Among the unusual business activities of the state are Benson's Wild Animal Farm, which supplies zoos and circuses all over the world, and a number of kennels breeding sled dogs. The dogs used on Admiral Byrd's Antarctic expeditions came from Chinook Kennels near Tomworth.

Mineral production in New Hampshire is relatively small, with only two states producing less. The principal mineral products are sand and gravel, stone, mica, and feldspar. The total annual mineral value is about fifteen million dollars, forty-eighth among the states.

Relatively little of New Hampshire's land is suitable for farming.

A New England "sugaring off," 1845, *painted by T.H. Matteson.*

In spite of this, the state's farmers make good use of all available land and annually produce nearly one hundred million dollars worth of farm products. Dairying is most important among agricultural activities, followed by poultry.

## TRANSPORTATION AND COMMUNICATION

New Hampshire and Massachusetts shared an early and notable "first" in transportation. In 1761 the first regular stage run in America was commenced between Boston and Portsmouth. However, most early overland travel was difficult. Lady Wentworth, wife of Royal Governor John Wentworth, had an interesting comment on travel in those days: "You may easily think I dread the journey, from the roughness of the carriage, as the roads are so bad and I, as great a coward as ever existed.... The Governor would attempt, and effect if possible, to ride over the tops of the trees on

Moose Mountain, while I even tremble at passing through a road cut at the foot of it. . . The roads are so precarious in the winter that it is impossible. . . I hope the roads will be better next year.''

To improve transportation, various enterprising people built toll roads or turnpikes. The first of these turnpikes in New Hampshire was built in 1796 from the coast to the east bank of the Merrimack River at Concord.

The Connecticut River had been bridged even before that time, however. Colonel Enoch Hale completed this bridge in 1785. A newspaper of the time wrote, ''This bridge is thought to exceed any bridge ever built in America in strength, elegance, and public utility as it is in the throughway from Boston through New Hampshire and Vermont to Canada.''

One of the country's most famous roads was finished in 1861, and on August 8 the first traffic was able to make a historic carriage drive to the summit of Mt. Washington. In its day, this mountain road was considered a wonder of the engineering world, and many would classify it as that even today. Although only 8 miles (12.9 kilometers) long, it ascends 4,700 feet (1,433 meters).

Today's roads are engineering marvels that carry four lanes of traffic over the shoulders of mountains, across rushing rivers, and whisk cars through once impossible mountain passes. New Hampshire Turnpike, Spaulding Turnpike, Everett Turnpike, and Interstate 89, 93, and 95 rank high among today's super roads.

The Kancamagus Highway, hailed as one of the ''most scenic roads of the East,'' was completed through the White Mountains between Conway and Lincoln in 1959.

The Merrimack River was opened to water traffic as far north as Concord by a series of locks and canals. Samuel Blodgett invested all of his wealth in a canal to circle Amoskeag Falls at Manchester, and there were six canals in all on the route. A steamboat had steamed up the Merrimack as early as 1814, but regular steamboat service did not begin between Lowell and Nashua until 1834. Extensive steamboat service followed.

Through a series of three canals, the Connecticut River was opened to flatboats. An account of 1816 relates that ''The Connecticut River is navigable two hundred and fifty miles (402 kilometers) above Hartford (Connecticut), for boats above fifteen tons (13.6 metric tons) and fifty miles (80 kilometers) higher for floats and pine timber."

The Boston and Maine Railroad was the first railroad to operate in New Hampshire. In 1849 it began running service between Exeter and Haverhill, Massachusetts. It reached Dover the next year. Gradually, railroads took over most of the heavy hauling of the state. Even today there are less than 1,000 miles (1,609 kilometers) of railroad tracks in New Hampshire.

One of the most imaginative projects in New Hampshire history was conceived by Sylvester Marsh of Littleton, a New Hampshire native, who had made his fortune in Chicago, Illinois. In 1855 Marsh asked the state legislature for a charter to build a railroad to the top of Mt. Washington. The reports say that the legislators burst into loud laughter. One of them offered an amendment to permit "Crazy Marsh" to extend his railroad to the moon. However, they finally gave Marsh the permission he wanted.

The plan was to add a kind of ratchet arrangement between the two regular tracks. Cog wheels on the engine would make a non-slip contact with the ratchet to propel the train up the mountain and keep it from sliding down the steep slopes. The funny little engine was devised by Walter Aiken of Franklin.

Financial difficulties and the Civil War delayed the project. Finally in 1866 Marsh himself financed a short demonstration section, built on the slopes of the mountain. It was such a success that the scoffers stayed to cheer, and capitalists gave him the necessary backing. On the world's first cog railroad, the first engine, called the *Hero* and nicknamed "Old Peppersass," was greeted at the summit with welcoming shouts in 1869. Marsh was called on to build similar railroads in many parts of the world.

Mount Washington even had its own newspaper for a time—published right on the top, called *Among the Clouds.*

The first newspaper published in New Hampshire was the New Hampshire *Gazette,* begun at Portsmouth in 1756. This is said to be the oldest continuously published newspaper in the country.

*George P.A. Healey's portrait of Franklin Pierce.*

# Human Treasures

## MR. PRESIDENT

In a log cabin at Hillsborough Lower Village on November 23, 1804, a boy was born who was destined to win the highest office his country could offer. This was Franklin Pierce, whose father was a veteran of the Revolutionary War. When Franklin was twenty-three years old his father became governor of New Hampshire.

The son studied and practiced law and also became a newspaper man—owner of one of the country's best-known small papers, the Concord *Monitor-Patriot.* He was speaker of the state legislature, then a United States congressman and finally a United States senator.

When the United States went to war with Mexico in 1846, Pierce enlisted and was wounded at Contreras. He held the rank of brigadier general when discharged.

The Democratic Party met in convention in 1852. The conflict that was bringing the country toward war made it almost impossible for all factions to decide on a candidate. At last, after forty-eight weary ballots, the convention, on the forty-ninth ballot, finally nominated Franklin Pierce as its candidate for president, and he was elected.

Although Pierce opposed slavery, there were many who said he was under the control of the pro-slavery forces. He made Jefferson Davis his secretary of war, and he approved the Kansas-Nebraska Act. During the Pierce administration, Admiral Peary opened Japan to the outside world, and the boundaries of the United States were extended through the Gadsden Purchase in 1853. Because of his "pro-slavery" policies, he was not renominated.

At Amherst in 1834 Pierce had married Jane Means Appleton, a native of Hampton. Their family life was to know much tragedy. They had three children; one died as an infant; another died at four, and the third was killed in a railway accident at the age of eleven.

Pierce was a strong supporter of President Andrew Jackson, who came to visit him at Concord where he then lived. The Hillsborough Center band was a notable musical organization. It was invited to serenade the president and traveled by wagon, reaching Concord at night. They struck up a lively tune, waking up the president. The future president, Franklin Pierce, was furious at the disturbance of his distinguished guest; he raved and ranted. However, President Jackson only laughed and invited the band to attend a banquet.

Franklin Pierce died in his beloved New Hampshire at Concord on October 8, 1869.


## THE "GODLIKE" DANIEL

Daniel Webster has been called New Hampshire's "greatest native son," and to many admiring New Englanders he was known as the "godlike" Daniel.

Daniel Webster was born at Franklin (then called Salisbury) on January 18, 1782. He began his practice of law at Portsmouth in 1807. His speech against the War of 1812, known as the "Rockingham Memorial," paved the way for his entrance into politics. During his career he served as a member of Congress from New Hampshire, and senator from Massachusetts on two different occasions.

He tried for the Whig presidential nomination in 1836 and 1840, but failed to gain this either time. Webster served as secretary of state under Presidents William Henry Harrison and John Tyler, also at a later date under Millard Fillmore. One of his most important accomplishments was the Webster-Ashburton Treaty of 1842, which defined the long-disputed northeastern boundary of the United States with Canada, including that of his native New Hampshire.

Daniel Webster was almost fanatically devoted to the preservation of the Union, and he probably sacrificed any chance he might have had to be president by being so outspoken against any forces he thought were threatening to break up his country.

Daniel Webster was renowned as one of the country's great constitutional lawyers and won many famous cases. He is usually also considered one of the greatest orators the country has ever produced. One of his best-known speeches was the 7th of March speech, in which he thundered: "I wish to speak today, not as a Massachusetts man, nor as a northern man, but as an American. . . I speak today for the preservation of the Union. 'Hear me for my cause.' "

He died October 24, 1852.

Among the interesting stories about Webster are those also concerning his brother Ezekiel. Daniel taught school to help finance his brother's education and when someone gave Daniel a horse, it provided transportation to Boston. He sold the horse to pay his board bill. When Ezekiel graduated, Daniel found him a law clerk's job, and he supported the two brothers while Daniel studied law.

Earlier Daniel had attended Phillips Exeter Academy at Exeter, a farm boy wearing outgrown clothes. The owner of his boarding house, Ebenezer Clifford, wanted to help Daniel with his table manners, which Clifford found crude and shocking, but he knew how sensitive the young man was. Finally Clifford worked out a plan with his assistant to make the same mistakes in manners as Daniel made. Clifford could then correct the assistant, and Daniel would get the point.

Another story is told of an even earlier period in Webster's life when someone gave Daniel a handkerchief on which the Constitution of the United States was printed. Whenever he had a free minute from his chores, he studied his "handkerchief."

Plymouth remembers itself as the place where Daniel Webster lost his first case. His client was so obviously guilty of murder that about all the young attorney could do was to argue against the wickedness of capital punishment.


## OTHER PUBLIC FIGURES

Horace Greeley was born at Amherst on February 3, 1811. He founded several publications and finally started the New York *Tribune*. As the publisher and editor of the *Tribune*, he became one of the world's best-known newspapermen.

Through his newspaper, Greeley was able to exert great influence in favor of his opinions, especially in the North and West. He is supposed to have originated the phrase "Go West, young man," but actually he borrowed it from an assistant.

In 1872 he ran as the Liberal Republican candidate for president, but Ulysses S. Grant's great popularity was too much for any opponent. Horace Greeley died in New York November 29, 1872.

One of the interesting little stories told about Horace Greeley in the region of his birth was that he learned to read while he was very young. He gained this skill while sitting on his mother's knee and looking at the books she was reading. However, because of the angle at which he was sitting, little Horace first learned to read upside down. Tradition says that he had finished reading the Bible by the time he was four years old.

Among the many prominent families of New Hampshire were the Chases. At one time one of the Chase family is said to have boasted to one of the also numerous Bellows family that there were enough members of his family to "Chase" all the Bellows out of the state. The Bellows representative quickly retorted that there were enough "Bellows" to blow them all back.

The most prominent Chase was Salmon Portland Chase, born at Claremont in 1808. A graduate of Dartmouth, and an attorney, he gained fame in defending fugitive slaves and as an organizer of the Liberty and Free Soil parties. He served in the United States Senate on two separate occasions and also was governor of Ohio. He was an unsuccessful candidate for president in 1860 and became Lincoln's secretary of the treasury, where his policies helped the Union remain financially solvent during the war.

Lincoln appointed him Chief Justice of the United States in 1864. In this post he was the judge at the trial of Jefferson Davis and presided over the impeachment trial of President Andrew Johnson. He died in 1873.

Another prominent New Hampshire family, the Wentworths, first gained fame as early royal governors.

Governor Benning Wentworth was long remembered for the party he gave in his mansion at Portsmouth on his sixtieth birthday, with most of the leaders of colonial society present. After a sumptuous banquet, the governor brought out his housekeeper, Martha Hilton,

*Salmon Portland Chase, the most prominent member of the Chase family.*

and called on the rector of the local church, the Reverend Arthur Brown, to marry them. No one, bride, guests, or minister, had any advance warning of the wedding. However, as soon as the minister could recover his composure, he conducted the proper ceremony before the astonished guests.

The poet Longfellow used this story as the basis for his work called *Lady Wentworth,* said by some to be "charming but inaccurate."

Benning Wentworth is supposed to have been rather insecure about how long his powers would last, although he ruled from 1741 to 1767. At the back of the house is said to have been a dock where the governor's sloop was moored, always ready for a hasty escape. Fast horses were rumored to be constantly at hand in the basement of the mansion. They were never used for flight. Benning Wentworth died in his mansion in 1770.

A later member of the Wentworth family who gained great prominence was John Wentworth of Sandwich. A graduate of Dartmouth, he went to Chicago and became a newspaper publisher there. He later went to Congress but gained his greatest fame as mayor of Chicago. Because of his height he was given the nickname "Long

John" Wentworth. It is reported that he contributed the city's first fire engine to Chicago. He later wrote *A History of the Wentworth Family in Europe and America.*

Among New Hampshire's other prominent people were Henry Wilson, vice-president of the United States from 1873 to 1875, who was born at Farmington, and John Parker Hale of Dover, called "one of the state's most distinguished men." John Adams Dix, native of Boscowen, served as a United States senator, secretary of the treasury, governor of New York, and a general of the Civil War.

Many other prominent military men have been associated with the state.

Before General John Stark died at Manchester in 1822 at the age of ninety-three, he was the last living general of the Revolutionary War. A native of Londonderry, as a young man he was taken prisoner by the Indians while he and his famous Derryfield (Manchester) men were fighting in the Indian wars. He was carried off to Canada but eventually ransomed.

General Stark became one of the principal leaders of the Revolutionary War, playing key parts in two decisive battles. As soon as the bonfires were lighted on the New Hampshire highlands to announce the first fighting of the Revolution, John Stark was off to Boston, gathering recruits along the way. A good percentage of the Americans at the Battle of Bunker Hill were from New Hampshire, and Stark's men are credited with much of the gallantry that almost turned a retreat into a victory.

General Stark took part in the battles of Princeton and Trenton but resigned because he was not promoted. However, when he heard of enemy General Burgoyne's sweep into New Hampshire, he hurried to the front and was probably most responsible for the American success at the Battle of Bennington. This battle may have weakened Burgoyne sufficiently to have caused his later final defeat at Saratoga.

Revolutionary War General John Sullivan of Durham was also governor (then called president) of New Hampshire from 1786 to 1790. He was one of the most urgent seekers of independence and wrote to John Adams in 1775, "Let me ask if we have anything to hope from his Majesty or his Ministers. Have we any encouragement from the people of Great Britain? Could they exert themselves more if we had shaken off the yoke and declared ourselves independent? Why, then, in God's name is it not done?... Do they (the Continental Congress) think the fate of Charlestown or Falmouth might have been worse, or the King's proclamation more severe, if we had openly declared War? Could they have treated our prisoners worse had we been in open and avowed rebellion than they do now?''

The story is told that before John Sullivan's mother left for America, a friend asked why she would make such a journey from her native Ireland. ''Raise governors for thim, to be sure,'' she retorted. John Sullivan's father saw her get off the boat, was struck by her appearance, paid her fare, later married her, and they did eventually have a governor for a son.

Another prominent Revolutionary figure was General Lewis Cass, native of Exeter. He gained later fame as first governor of the Northwest Territory. Colonel Alexander Scammell of Durham was adjutant general for George Washington.


## SUCH INVENTIVE PEOPLE

New Hampshire people have been noted for their success in making do with what they have and for their ingenuity.

One of these was Jonas Chickering, native of Greenville. In the piano-making firm that he founded, he devised the first cast metal frame to hold piano strings tightly and keep them in tune. He also greatly improved the existing methods of piano stringing.

John Morrill, who was born at Boscowen, gained fame as the inventor of the eight-day clock. Isaac Adams of Sandwich completely changed the printing industry by finding a way to attach engines to printing presses, becoming the ''father'' of the power press.

Walter Aiken of Franklin produced a comparatively simple item but one which has been vital in working with metal. This was the hacksaw. Another ''cutting'' device, hair clippers, was first produced by inventors J.K. Priest and R.T. Smith.

Elias Howe is considered to have perfected the sewing machine while working on his invention at Nashua, and Dr. Charles Greeley Abbott of Wilton is the inventor of the solar motor.

Thaddeus S.C. Lowe was one of the country's pioneer balloonists. John H. Gage of Nashua built the first machine lathe in the country and founded the first company to make machine tools.

Two leaders in widely differing businesses were Peter Wilder, New Ipswich manufacturer of a noted type of chair, and Pierce Cheney, native of Hillsborough Lower Village, who became a principal figure in the creation of the Santa Fe Railroad.


## SUCH CREATIVE PEOPLE

New Hampshire gained a reputation of leadership in the promotion of culture through the efforts of one of America's most renowned and respected composers of music and through the dedication of his wife. After gaining great fame as a pianist as well as composer, in 1895 Edward MacDowell purchased an old farm at Peterborough. He and his wife, Marian Nevins MacDowell, had a dream of making this a haven where creative people might come and have the time and quiet they needed to do their best work.

After MacDowell died in 1908, Marian MacDowell toured the country tirelessly, playing concerts of MacDowell compositions to raise funds for the Edward MacDowell Association that she had formed. She began to build studios on the farm at Peterborough, and eventually the farm became known as the MacDowell Colony.

Here came artists in all fields, those who had already gained fame and those who were still unknown. Among those who accomplished much at the colony and brought artistic fame to New Hampshire were Edwin Arlington Robinson, Willa Cather, Mabel Daniels, Louis Untermeyer, Thornton Wilder, Stephen Vincent Benet, Roy Harris, Aaron Copland, Edgar Stillman Kelley, and Charles Wakefield Cadman.

Mrs. MacDowell continued her activity and interest in the colony until her death in 1956 at the age of ninety-nine.

56

*Mrs. MacDowell at the piano at the Colony.*

Another prominent New Hampshire concert pianist and famed woman composer was Mrs. H.H.A. Beach of Hillsborough.

Walter Kittredge, born at Reed's Ferry, gave the country one of its best-known and best-loved wartime songs when he composed *Tenting on the Old Camp Ground.*

Among the unusual musicians of the state were the Hutchinson Family group—thirteen brothers and sisters of Milford, who gained a reputation in extensive singing tours.

In 1885 renowned sculptor Augustus Saint-Gaudens was working on his *Standing Lincoln.* When someone told him he would find plenty of "Lincoln-shaped" men in the Cornish, New Hampshire, region, he set up a studio there and became one of the most enthusiastic boosters of the state.

Saint-Gaudens attracted to New Hampshire many students who later became famous. Among these were Maxfield Parrish, who established a permanent home near Plainfield, Frederick William MacMonnies, and Charles Dana Gibson. In 1907 Augustus Saint-Gaudens died on his porch at Aspet, as the sun began to set behind Mount Ascutney. His last words have become quite well known: "It is very beautiful, but I want to go farther away."

Another world-renowned sculptor, a native of Exeter, was Daniel Chester French, whose best-known work is the giant statue of Lincoln in the memorial at Washington.

A modern artist who had a prominent association with New Hampshire was the internationally renowned Mexican mural painter, Jose Clemente Orozco, who joined the teaching staff at Dartmouth, and painted controversial murals there.

Many of the greatest names in American literature have been associated with New Hampshire.

Nathaniel Hawthorne died at Plymouth in 1864. His writings often deal with New Hampshire scenes, and his work *The Great Stone Face* made that prominent feature of scenery widely known.

In 1892 John Greenleaf Whittier died in New Hampshire, at Hampton Falls, a region that had been the home of his ancestors. He wrote many of his poems in the region of West Ossipee, where he spent several summers. He was sometimes pestered by the summer visitors who liked to say they had met the great man. The poet spoke of one of these: "He extravagantly praised my work and all the time he called me Whittaker."

Whittier's poems written in or about New Hampshire include his lyric *The Birches of Lee, The Voyage of the Jettie, Among the Hills,* and *Sunset on the Bear Camp.*

The forests of New Hampshire were the inspiration for one of the best beloved of all nature poems. Joyce Kilmer was visiting at Swanzey. Staring at the beautiful foliage about him, he suddenly had an impulse to write and quickly jotted down a verse on a paper bag. This was his immortal *Trees.*

Beloved modern poet Robert Frost wrote in 1938: ". . . Nearly half of my poems must actually have been written in New Hampshire.

Every single person in my 'North of Boston' was friend or acquaintance of mine in New Hampshire. I lived, somewhat brokenly to be sure, in Salem, Derry, Plymouth and Franconia, New Hampshire, from my tenth to my forty-fifth year. Most of my time out of it I lived in Lawrence, Massachusetts, on the edge of New Hampshire, where my walks and vacations could be in New Hampshire. My first teaching was in a district school in the southern part of Salem, New Hampshire. Four of my children were born in Derry, New Hampshire. My father was born in Kingston, New Hampshire. My wife's mother was born in New Hampshire. So you see it has been New Hampshire with me all the way. You will find my poems show it, I think." In later life, of course, he moved to neighboring Vermont.

Tabitha Gilman of Exeter is credited with being the earliest woman of America to write and publish a novel. This was her book *Female Quixotism.*

Winston Churchill, another American novelist, not the great British statesman, lived in Cornish and wrote many of his works there. His *Coniston* was partly based on his experience in New Hampshire politics. He was a candidate for governor in 1912. Probably his best-known work is *The Crisis.*

Even English novelist Charles Dickens wrote about the New Hampshire scene. One of his works is known as *The Fisherman of Sunapee.*

Among New Hampshire poets, Sam Walter Foss of Candia Depot is probably best known for his well-loved work *House by the Side of the Road.*


## SUCH INTERESTING PEOPLE

Of the prominent women born in New Hampshire no one is better known than Mary Baker Eddy, native of Bow, revered by her followers as the discoverer and founder of the Christian Science faith. She established the permanent form of the church's organization while living at Concord.

One of New Hampshire's most popular legends concerns "Ocean-Born Mary." Sometime in the 1700s pirates captured a ship, and a baby girl was born soon after to one of the captive women. The pirate captain asked to name the baby for his dead wife Mary, and the parents agreed. He and his men overwhelmed the baby with gifts and let the ship go on its way. Little Mary and her parents later settled in Londonderry. At her wedding to James Wallace, Mary was a famous bride for she wore a dress made from a piece of silk that was one of the presents given her by the pirates. Mary Wallace, who was always known as Ocean-Born Mary, lies buried in the Henniker Quaker cemetery, and her ghost is said to haunt her old home in Henniker.

Indian woman Molly Ocket gained fame by uncovering an Indian plot to kill Colonel Clark of Boston on one of his trips to the Conway region to trade for furs. Molly made a long and hard trip overland on foot and reached the colonel just in time to warn him and save his life.

Other notable Indians of New Hampshire included Metallak, last chief of the Coosuc; Chief Kancamagus, for whom the mountain is named; and the most renowned of all—Passaconaway—who had his headquarters on the site of Manchester.

One of the most unfortunate was Chief Massasecum. He saw

*Mary Baker Eddy, used by permission of the Christian Science Board of Directors.*

more clearly than other Indian leaders that the Europeans were too numerous and too strong to be beaten and that the Indians must eventually lose out. He suggested that his group make peace with the invaders, but for this his own people labeled him a coward and drove Massasecum and his family into exile. Although he tried to make friends with the Europeans, they would not have anything to do with him either. His wife and baby died, and he lived a lonely life in the woods until his life too came to an end.

More "fortunate" was Amos Fortune, a former slave who settled in Jaffrey and amassed considerable property. He was known throughout the state for his philanthropy.

A White Mountain pioneer was Ethan Allen Crawford, who established an inn near Fabyan. His wife wrote about how Crawford helped in the naming of the northern peaks: "This summer there came a considerable large party of distinguished characters . . . to my house about noon, to ascend the mountains and give names to such hills as were unnamed. . . I was loaded equal to a packhorse. [When they came to the summit] they gave names to several peaks and then drank healths to them in honor of the great men whose names they bore, and gave toasts to them."

Another of the great "boosters" of the White Mountain region and one of the best-known authorities on the area was the very popular Reverend Thomas Starr King. In 1859 he wrote his classic book *The White Hills: Their Legends, Landscapes, and Poetry.*

A well-known account of another region far removed from New Hampshire was written by John Ledyard of Portsmouth. This restless globetrotter joined Captain Cook, and John Ledyard wrote the only eyewitness story of the death of Captain Cook on his visit to Hawaii.

Among those who accomplished feats of some kind or other, the accomplishment of John Lovewell should be noted. He was famous for attending church regularly at the age of one hundred. Nor will New Hampshire people probably want to forget Lemuel F. Cooper of Grantham, whose prize hog grew to weigh 1,000 pounds (454 kilograms), after which it was stuffed and exhibited to admiring throngs at the Philadelphia world's fair in 1876.

*Dartmouth College*

# Teaching and Learning

New Hampshire's famous Dartmouth had possibly the most unusual beginning of any of the nation's great institutions of higher learning. The Reverend Eleazar Wheelock had directed a school for Indians in Connecticut, but he wanted a change of location and better financing.

He sent one of his converts, a remarkable Indian named Samson Occom, to England to preach and raise money. Occom made such a profound impression upon the people in England that he soon raised the remarkable sum of eleven thousand pounds sterling. King George III provided a charter in 1769, "for the education & instruction of Youth of the Indian Tribes in this Land in reading, writing & all parts of Learning which shall appear necessary and expedient for civilizing and Christianizing Children of Pagans as well as in all liberal Arts and Sciences; and also of English Youth and any others."

Locations for the college were offered by the colonies from Virginia to New Hampshire, but Wheelock selected a 3,000-acre (1,214-hectare) site provided by the twenty families then living in Hanover, New Hampshire. After a time, the main purpose of training Indian young people was changed to general education for all. There were four men in the first graduating class of 1771. One of these was John Wheelock, son of the president, who became president on the death of his father. In order to attend the first graduation, Governor John Wentworth had a new road built for 75 miles (121 kilometers) through the wilderness from Wolfeboro. The road was not entirely finished until 1772.

The governor, with surprising modesty, refused to let the college be named for him; instead he suggested that it be named for one of the most enthusiastic of the English supporters, the Earl of Dartmouth, and this was done. The governor presented some valuable lands to the university, along with grants to each member of the graduating class. He presented a silver punchbowl to Dr. Wheelock, and this is used to the present day. The governor also gave the president a very elaborate badge as a symbol of his office. This still is proudly passed on from one president of Dartmouth to the next.

Dartmouth, the nation's ninth oldest college, celebrated its two hundredth birthday in 1969. It combines New England small-town surroundings with cultural advantages normally associated with great metropolitan centers. It restricts its entering classes to limited numbers and 70 percent of its graduates go on to advanced studies. The three-term undergraduate curriculum established in 1958 offers seven hundred courses. Graduate-level training is offered in business, engineering, medicine, and other fields.

The University of New Hampshire also had its start at Hanover when the New Hampshire College of Agriculture and the Mechanic Arts was established there. In 1892 Benjamin Thompson left five hundred thousand dollars to the state to establish a college of agriculture on his Durham farm, and the college was moved to Durham in 1893.

From that time on it grew rapidly, and in 1923 the name was changed to the University of New Hampshire. Today the main campus of 1,700 (688 hectares) acres with more than fifty buildings provides for students enrolled in four colleges and a fast-growing graduate school at Henniker. Its Engineering Experiment Station is particularly noteworthy. State colleges at Keene and Plymouth are now in the state university system.

A center for continuing education, made possible by a grant from the Kellogg Foundation, is located at Durham to serve the six state universities of New England.

Other colleges of the state include Colby-Sawyer, New London; Franconia College; Franklin Pierce College, Rindge; Mount Saint Mary College, Hooksett; Nathaniel Hawthorne College, Antrim; New England College, Henniker; Rivier College, Nashua; and St. Anselm's College and Notre Dame College, both at Manchester.

Some of the nation's most notable preparatory schools are located in New Hampshire.

John Phillips, wealthy Exeter man, already had founded Phillips Academy in Massachusetts, but his interest in education was such that he also gave liberally to provide in 1781 another school in his own community, and this became famed Phillips Exeter Academy. Over the years it has given an educational foundation to many

64

famous men, including Daniel Webster and the sons of three presidents: Robert Todd Lincoln, Ulysses S. Grant Jr., and Richard and Francis Cleveland. One of the high points in Phillips Exeter history was the visit of Abraham Lincoln to his son while he studied at Exeter.

In one hundred eighty-five years of history, Phillips Exeter had only ten principals to administer its renowned system of education; this is now known as the Harkness Roundtable, carried on by a faculty of outstanding teachers with results that are studied worldwide.

Other well-known names in preparatory education are Tilton School at Tilton and St. Paul's School, Concord. Because of its large endowment, St. Paul's, an Episcopal school, is able to offer many advantages to its students. Brewster Academy was chartered in 1820 to offer an education to all regardless of "age, sex, color." The school aims to prepare its students for college in a way that will make them appreciate the traditional New England principles of hard work, fair play, honesty, and integrity.

The first New England act on education in 1642 encouraged local communities to sponsor schools. By 1647 each town of fifty or more population was required to maintain a school because: "It being one chiefe project of that ould deluder, Sathan, to keepe men from the knowledge of the Scripture as in former times, by keeping them in an unknowne tongue, so in these latter times . . . that learning may not be buried in the grave of our fathers. . . . "

The first public high school in New Hampshire was established at Portsmouth in 1830. The statewide system of schools now in effect was established in 1919.

A notable New Hampshire contribution to general education was the Juvenile Library of Dublin, established in 1822, said to be the earliest free public library in the United States.

*Winter on the summit of Mt. Washington.*

# Enchantment of New Hampshire

One of nature's most spectacular displays reaches its greatest perfection in New Hampshire, and those world travelers who have not yet experienced the blazing—almost blistering—colors of the New Hampshire autumn have been saving the best for last. To see New Hampshire at the height of its color is an experience that cannot be duplicated anywhere else in the world. Other states are noted for their fall foliage, but the red, yellow, and orange colors set against the dark green perfection of the evergreens of New Hampshire's mountainsides are the most brilliant and vivid of all. Hues that seem highly exaggerated in pictures and colored slides of New Hampshire autumn are really true.

Other attractions of the state range from salt-water fishing and boating to many major snow skiing areas. Attractions of some of the country's finest lake and mountain resorts and state parks are combined with the quaintness of rural New Hampshire, with its traditions of the country store, a few of which may yet be found, along with about sixty remaining covered bridges. These are jealously protected by the New Hampshire Covered Bridge Association.

## MOUNTAIN WONDERLAND

"This is the second greatest show on earth," exclaimed P.T. Barnum from the top of Mount Washington. If he had not been prejudiced about his circus being the "greatest show on earth," Barnum might well have given that title to the majestic panorama of the White Mountains.

The first man to climb Mr. Washington was Darby Fields in 1642. When he came back, he claimed the mountains were full of valuable gems. Small quantities of gold were discovered in some regions such as Lisbon, and the largest piece of pure galena (lead) ever mined came from the Gorham region, but for the most part the value of the mountains lay in their primeval forests and in their beauty.

Mt. Washington gained its name when the Reverend Manasseh

Cutler christened it in 1784 on his scientific expedition. In 1832 this magnificent peak was a part of a piece of land purchased for only three hundred dollars. It was left to Dartmouth by Colonel Teague and was later purchased by the state.

Mt. Washington has been the scene of some strange "records." Harlan P. Amen, Phillips Exeter Academy principal, ran down the whole distance in 1875 in a record 54 minutes. A woman weighing 230 pounds (104 kilograms) took a one thousand dollar bet and hiked to the summit in 1885. She walked back the same day and danced that evening in the Glen House.

The first women to climb Mt. Washington were the Misses Austin; they made the climb with White Mountain authority Ethan Allen Crawford, who was so lame at the time that he had to make the climb using a cane.

At the top of Mt. Washington is Summit House, a resort hotel. From here the whole panorama of the White Mountains is unfolded, from the ocean on the east and Canada on the north to Massachusetts in the south and past Vermont into New York on the west.

Possibly the best-known single feature of the mountain region is *The Old Man of the Mountain.* The first-known written description of the profile appeared in the Concord *Register* in 1826: "[I] had heard stories of such a wonder in these parts—did not believe there was any—thought there might be something there that could be tortured into a profile but nothing like this—perfect face—astonishing—looks like an old warrior with a helmet—... a petrifaction of some of the Titans who lived ... when there were 'giants in the earth.'"

Although he looks tiny from the highway and from Profile Lake, the Old Man actually extends for 48 feet (14.6 meters) from chin's bottom to the top of the brow. Nathaniel Hawthorne exaggerated its size when he wrote in *The Great Stone Face,* "It seemed as if an enormous giant or titan had sculptured his own likeness on the precipice. There was the broad arch of the forehead, a hundred feet (30 meters) in height, the nose, with its long bridge; and the vast lips, which, if they could have spoken, would have rolled their thunder accents from one end of the valley to the other."

Poet John Greenleaf Whittier spoke of how "The great Notch

68

mountains shone, watched over by the solemn-browed and awesome face of stone.''

Not so well known is a neighbor of the Old Man—the Old Woman of the Notch, looking down from Eagle Cliff with stern gaze, topped by a shock of hair made up of bushes and trees.

Not far from the Old Man is another attraction of the popular Franconia Notch area—the Flume—a scenic canyon formed by the carving of Flume Brook. The Flume is supposed to have been discovered by ninety-three-year-old Aunt Jess Guernsey who was looking for a new fishing spot.

One of the main resorts of the White Mountain area is Bethlehem,

*Cannon Mt. aerial tramway, Franconia Notch.*

headquarters of the American Hay Fever Association. From Bethlehem President Ulysses S. Grant is said to have "taken the wildest ride of his life," to see *The Old Man of the Mountain.* The coach driver, Edmund Cox, got the best horses available and made the two-hour drive in the record time of fifty-eight minutes. According to Alice B. Stevens, "It was all Cox could do to manage them [the horses]... Their ears pricked up, their eyes full of fire, nipping and striking at each other... The General's keen eyes recognized at once the quality of the horses and he stepped up to the driver and asked, 'If you haven't any objection, I will ride up here with you.' Cox said, 'It's pretty rough riding up here, General,' but the President said, 'I can stand it if you can,' and clambered up."

The distance was supposed to require two hours; Bethlehem wired the Profile House when the party left at seven o'clock. Miss Stevens continues by quoting Ben Daniel of the Notch: "Well, 'long 'bout 8 o'clock we had got word that they was on the road. The crowd of us stood near the hotel, talkin' and waitin', when all of a sudden, bang went the cannon! The guests all run out on the piazza. We looked at each other, and we looked at our watches and we said, 'It can't be.' But it was, for we could hear the clatter of the horses' hoofs comin' and before we heard the second cannon, everbody was shouting, 'Here they come, clear the road!' and in a flash, they were right on us, Cox holdin' the lines drawn hard up and General Grant beside him, holdin' onto his hat with one hand and to the seat with the other. The President, when he got down from the box, was a curious sight, covered with dust from head to foot."

Miss Stevens also quoted Simon Thayer of the Notch: "S'pose you've heard tell that them hosses run ever inch of the road. Well, they didn't, not by my galluses they didn't. They just floo, actooly floo over the road, half the time the wheels of that stage were just spinnin' in the air when they rounded the curves."

Grant is reported to have sent Cox a coach whip for a present the next Christmas, and this is now displayed at the New Hampshire Historical Society, Concord.

One of the best-known stories of the mountains is that of the tragic Willey family. Nathaniel Hawthorne tells the sad tale of what

70

happened one night at their cabin under ominous-looking Frankenstein Cliff in Crawford Notch: "The house and all within it trembled; the foundations of the earth seemed to be shaken as if this awful sound were the peal of the last trump. Young and old exchanged one wild glance, and remained an instant, pale, affrighted, without utterance, or power to move. Then the same shriek burst simultaneously from all their lips.

" 'The Slide! The Slide!'

"The simplest words must intimate, but not portray, the unutterable horror of the catastrophe. The victims rushed from their cottage, and sought refuge in what they deemed a safer spot—where in contemplation of such an emergency, a sort of barrier had been reared. Alas! they had quitted their security, and fled right into the pathway of destruction. Down came the whole side of the mountain, in a cataract of ruin. Just before it reached the house, the stream (avalanche) broke into two branches—shivered not a window there but overwhelmed the whole vicinity. . . . Their bodies were never found. . . . The next morning, the light smoke was seen stealing from the cottage chimney up the mountainside. Within, the fire was yet smouldering on the hearth, and the chairs in a circle round it, as if the inhabitants had but gone forth to view the devastation of the Slide, and would shortly return, to thank Heaven for their miraculous escape."

Hawthorne was not quite accurate. The bodies of the older Willeys and two of their children were found by Ethan Allen Crawford and buried at Intervale.

One of the principal highways of the mountains passes through picturesque Crawford Notch. This notch was first found in 1771 by Timothy Nash. When Governor Wentworth heard of this possible route through the mountains, he offered Nash a grant of land if the route was suitable for bringing a horse through. Nash won his land, with the help of a friend; they sometimes had to hoist the horse up or down steep places using ropes, but they got him through the notch.

Lost River, near North Woodstock, appears and disappears during a quarter-mile course. The region has been called "a geological wonderland," and a museum houses a rock and insect collection.

*A golf course in North Conway.*

Another of New Hampshire's scenic notches—Dixville Notch—is said to have one of the most impressive views of the state.

Pinkham Notch is noted for the Glen Ellis Falls Scenic Area and Tuckerman Ravine. The ravine is considered to be the only really "Alpine" type of ski area in the East. Another attraction of Pinkham Notch region is Snow Arch. This is formed when water cuts through the winter's heavy accumulations of snow, carving a long, high arch, which can be veiwed until it melts.

*Skiing on Mt. Bannon in Bartlett.*

At the south end of Pinkham Notch is one of the state's most picturesque mountain villages—Jackson. Joseph Pinkham, for whom the notch was named, came to this region in 1790. The story is told that all of his worldly possessions were hauled to Jackson on a sled pulled by the pet pig of the family.

Berlin was the site of the founding of possibly the oldest ski club in the country, the Nansen Club, founded in 1872. The Nansen Ski Jump near Berlin is the highest steel tower jump in the United States. Near Berlin is the Devil's Hop-Yard, a region of interesting rock formations, one of them looming high into the air.

## A BANK OF STRAWBERRIES: PORTSMOUTH

The passengers were starved for fresh fruit. Eagerly they went ashore when they saw that the riverbank was almost covered with a crimson carpet of ripe strawberries. They were so impressed with this windfall that they called their new settlement "Strawbery Banke." It later became the city of Portsmouth.

Today in an area of 10 acres (4 hectares) in that first part of the city Strawbery Banke, Inc., a non-profit organization, has taken over twenty-five aged buildings to restore the old town much as it was in the early days. Other old houses have been moved into the area, making the Strawbery Banke restoration one of the most important in the country.

Portsmouth is a city of famous old buildings. Historic St. John's Episcopal Church has what is said to be the oldest organ in the United States. An early churchgoer who did not believe in musical instruments called it "An ungodly chest of whistles." The church also prizes its copy of the so-called "Vinegar Bible," one of the few copies printed in which the word vineyard is misspelled "vinegar."

One of the most notable American houses is the Wentworth-Coolidge Mansion. Here Governor Benning Wentworth's famous wedding took place. This mansion and its setting of some 20 acres (8 hectares) on Little Harbor, with the island in the harbor, were given to the state of New Hampshire by Mrs. J. Templeman Coolidge.

Among the great Georgian houses of America is the Governor John Langdon Memorial. As president pro-tempore of the United States Senate, Langdon had the honor of notifying George Washington of his election as president. Langdon was five times governor of New Hampshire.

One of the most patriotic of men, during Washington's trials at Valley Forge, Governor Langdon declared: "I have one thousand dollars in hard money; I will pledge my plate for three thousand more, and I have seventy hogshead of Tobago Rum, which will be sold for the most they will bring. They are at the service of the state. If we succeed in defending our firesides and our homes, I may be remunerated; if we do not then the property will be of no value to me."

Other Portsmouth houses include the Jackson House; the so-called John Paul Jones House, occupied by the Portsmouth Historical Society; Moffatt-Ladd House; and the Warner House.

Portsmouth's famous harbor, with recent improvements, now provides a 4-mile (6-kilometer) channel up the Piscataqua River with a 35-foot (10.6-meter) channel depth, navigable for all but the largest ocean ships. The nearby Isles of Shoals abound in legend and history.

## CONCORD

The Concord Chamber of Commerce proclaims with pride that their city "became the birthplace of the United States on June 21, 1788, when as the ninth and deciding state, New Hampshire ratified the federal constitution and made it effective." The spot where this occurred is marked by a tablet.

Concord began in 1721 when certain residents of Haverhill, Massachusetts, asked for land where Concord now stands, in the following quaint petition: "Ye Petitioners being straitened for Accomodations for themselves and their posterity, have Espied a tract of land, scituate on the River of Merrimake, whereon they are desirous to make a settlement and form a town. . . ." The first settlement was in 1727, under the original town name of Penacook.

*The state capitol in Concord.*

Later called Concord, that town became the capital of New Hampshire in 1808, at which time the state capitol or statehouse was begun. Finished in 1819, it is built of granite from the Concord area and decorated with Vermont marble. The most interesting feature of the interior is the Hall of Flags, with flags preserved from the state's fighting forces beginning in Colonial days.

Here the state legislature, officially known as the General Court, meets. New Hampshire is noted for having the largest house of representatives of any state.

In the city's Civic Square there is a fine State Library of four hundred thousand volumes, the beautiful New Hampshire Historical Society with museum, library and lecture hall, and the City Auditorium.

The League of New Hampshire Arts and Crafts has its headquarters in Concord and provides a salesroom for New Hampshire craftsmen. Each year it holds a Craftsmen's Fair.


## MANCHESTER

For many years Manchester was almost a one-industry city, dominated by the mammoth Amoskeag Manufacturing Company. In the 1930s, when this giant company toppled into financial ruin, the situation was desperate, but a group of faithful citizens raised five million dollars to buy the plant. The people determined to revive the town, and they did. Now instead of depending on one industry, Manchester has about two hundred fifty and is rapidly growing.

Settlement began at Manchester in 1722. It was originally known as Old Harrytown and later as Tyngstown. Early determination of the Manchester settlers is shown by the fact that thirty-six of the thirty-eight able-bodied men of the area fought in the Battle of Bunker Hill.

The community name later became Derryfield, but in 1810 Judge Samuel Blodgett predicted that the tiny town of 615 people would become the "Manchester of New England." With the growth of the giant Amoskeag Company, this prediction came true, both in name and in deed.

One of the principal smaller museums of New England is the Currier Gallery of Art, a gift to the city of Governor and Mrs. Moody Currier. Its collection of New England decorative art is especially fine.

The museum of the Manchester Historic Association has many local displays, including a particularly interesting collection of patterns from the Amoskeag mills.


## HANOVER AND DARTMOUTH

A visitor to Hanover in the winter might think that he had suddenly entered a strange frozen world. When the Dartmouth Winter

Carnival is on, the campus sprouts gigantic snow sculpture, some statues 20 and 30 feet (6 and 9 meters) tall. There are also athletic contests and social events. The Winter Carnival is believed to be the oldest and largest of its type.

Hopkins Center at Dartmouth was opened in 1962, offering four art galleries, two theaters, a concert hall, and smaller recital halls as well as workshops. The center presents an annual Congregation of the Arts in July and August.

*The winter carnival at Dartmouth.*

Among the most controversial art works in the United States are the murals painted by Mexican artist Jose Clemente Orozco, in Baker Library at Dartmouth. The entire series of murals is based on Quetzalcoatl, worshipped as the Great White Father in Mexico.

One of the unusual institutions of Dartmouth is Dick's House, donated by Mr. and Mrs. Edwin K. Hall to honor their son Richard, who died in his sophomore year. To explain their gift, the Halls wrote: "The purpose of Dick's House is to provide a home for the boys of Dartmouth when they are sick or ailing. It is our hope that the boys will come to feel that 'going up to Dick's House' is the next best thing to going to their own homes when they are in need of either the care or the surroundings that the dormitory or fraternity house is unable to furnish."

In a book in Dick's House library is a poignant inscription by President Calvin Coolidge: "To Edwin K. Hall, in recollection of his son and my son who have the privilege by the grace of God to be boys through all eternity." Coolidge was referring to Calvin, Jr., who died at sixteen.

Dartmouth owns most of Mt. Moosilauke. The region provides 180 miles (290 kilometers) of trails for hiking and makes a particular specialty of winter sports. It maintains some especially fine ski lifts and trails for everyone from novice to expert.

Near Hanover is the Saint-Gaudens Museum at the home and studio of Augustus Saint-Gaudens. About a hundred works of the famous artist are on display there.


**THE REST OF THE STATE**

Joseph Scott wrote of Exeter in 1796: "Here are also ten grist mills, a paper mill, a fulling mill, a slitting mill, a snuff mill, two chocolate and six saw mills, iron works, a printing office and a duck manufactory...Previous to the Revolution this town was famous for ship building but latterly it has been much neglected."

Exeter remembers its "radical" past, including the nonconforming Reverend John Wheelwright and the heresy-banned Quaker

*A rural scene in Meriden.*

Anne Hutchinson, and Amos Tuck who suggested the name for the then radical Republican Party. But today the venerable and quiet city is known mostly for Phillips Exeter Academy.

Epping gained its principal fame as the home of three governors of New Hampshire, also of Henry Dearborn, United States secretary of war, and John Chandler, United States senator from Maine.

East Derry made an important contribution to education as the home of Adams Female Academy. This school set the pattern for much of the education of women that followed.

Nashua is New Hampshire's second city in population. The first settler was a man named Cromwell, in 1656. Other settlers arrived four years later. The region was first a trading post for furs, and the city's original name was Dunstable.

The Nashua River, dashing over Mine Falls, early provided power for much of Nashua's manufacturing. It is still noted for its manufacturing and as a trading center for a large area.

At Nashua lived John Lovewell, a supporter of Cromwell, who had to flee England when Charles II became king. At Lovewell's house Hannah Dustin found shelter in her escape from the Indians. Lovewell died in 1754, when it was thought he might have been as much as one hundred twenty years old.

Near Milford is Devil's Footprint, with its amusing legend. The story is told that the Devil was anxious to claim the people of the region as his own so he invited the men to a baked-bean dinner, with the beans to be cooked in his own bean pot, a large pothole still to be seen in the rocks. Just as he was dishing out the beans to the large number of guests, his foot sank into the rock that had become heated by the fire. His roars frightened away all the guests, and the mark of his footprint has been there ever since.

At New Boston is the Molly Stark Cannon, with its incredible story of "travel." It was brought to America from Paris in 1743, captured from General Burgoyne by General John Stark at the Battle of Bennington, used later in the War of 1812 at Detroit, captured by the British there, later retaken by the Americans at Fort George and finally returned to New Hampshire.

Appleton Academy at New Ipswich was the second established in New Hampshire. The distinguished Appleton family included Nathan, the founder of Lowell, Massachusetts; his daughter, who became the wife of Henry Wadsworth Longfellow; and Jesse, president of Bowdoin College; and his daughter, who was the wife of Franklin Pierce.

At Rindge is the Cathedral of the Pines, with its Altar of the Nation, a national memorial for all American war dead. Another unique war memorial is the statue *Buddies* hewn by Count Vigo Brandt Erickson from a 25-ton (22.6-metric ton) granite fieldstone, hauled from the foot of Mt. Monadnock. It stands in the East Jaffrey village center.

At Peterborough stands another kind of memorial—a living memorial to the devotion and faith of Mr. and Mrs. Edward Mac-

*The MacDowell Colony*

Dowell. Here is their famous foundation where both the prominent and little-known artists in every field have an opportunity to create under the best conditions.

The principal community of the Mt. Monadnock region is Keene. Keene Teachers College, now Keene State, is the largest of its type in New England. The city is noted for its Square and Folk Dance Festival.

The beginning of permanent settlement at Keene came in 1750.

82

Miss Fiske's Seminary for Young Ladies at Keene was the second of its kind ever founded in the United States.

The town of Washington is noted as being the second in the country (after Washington, North Carolina) to take the name of the Father of our Country. New Hampshire's Washington was incorporated in 1776.

Claremont gains distinction from its celebration of Russian Easter and Russian Christmas.

Near Cornish is the Saint-Gaudens National Historic Site, overlooking the Connecticut Valley. The largest building at the memorial is Aspet, the Saint-Gaudens home. Also open to the public are the Little Studio and the New Studio, built for the sculptor's work on the monument to General Sherman, on Fifth Avenue in New York. In this studio is the full-sized model of the *Standing Lincoln* now in Lincoln Park in Chicago.

*Silver Lake*

*Edward MacDowell's original studio at the MacDowell Colony.*

Near Plainfield Helen Woodruff Smith, a nature lover, bought and established the nature sanctuary, named in her honor—the first one of its kind in the country. A notable feature is the birdbath carved from a 5-ton (4.5-metric ton) boulder by Annetta Saint-Gaudens.

At Hillsborough the historic boyhood home of Franklin Pierce contains furniture, utensils, imported scenic wallpaper, and stenciled walls of the period.

Salisbury has an interesting memory of another president. Gallant James Monroe toured New England in 1817. On his way through

*Mt. Washington cog train on Jacob's Ladder.*

Salisbury someone said that the ladies of Salisbury would like to have him leave his carriage so they could get a better look at him. He hastened out of his coach, saying, "By gad, I'd like to see your ladies!"

Laconia stands at the entrance to New Hampshire's large and popular lake region. The city itself has a unique location on three lakes. Its winter carnival features the world championship sled-dog races. The Lake Winnipesaukee region is one of the leading resort areas of the country. Here in 1852 the first of the historic rowing races between Yale and Harvard was held. The first Guernsey cow ever brought to the United States was kept on Cow Island in the lake. The lake is dotted with islands, large and small; it backs up into many large and beautiful bays and because of its unusual shape seems to spread itself over a large area of the landscape. Almost every water sport of winter or summer can be found in the region.

Wolfeboro is the largest town on New Hampshire's largest lake. The city is also on Lake Wentworth, named for Governor Benning Wentworth, who built there the very first true "summer" home ever erected in the United States.

It is unfortunate that this Wentworth home burned in the early 1800s. Today it would be a fitting reminder that summer vacations were invented in this state, which is notable both for its wonderful vacations and its sturdy, inventive people.

# Handy Reference Section

## Instant Facts

Became the 9th state, June 21, 1788
Capital—Concord, settled 1727
Nickname—The Granite State
State motto—*Live Free or Die*
State bird—Purple finch *(Carpodacus purpureus)*
State tree—White birch *(Betula papyreifers)*
State flower—Purple lilac *(Syringa vulgaris)*
State songs—"Old New Hampshire," music by Maurice Hoffman, words by John
       F. Holmes; "New Hampshire, My New Hampshire," music by
       Walter P. Smith, words by Julius Richelson; and "New Hampshire
       Hills," music by Tom Powers, words by Paul Scott Mowrer
Area—9,304 square miles (24,097 square kilometers)
Rank in area—44th
Coastline—17.75 miles (30 kilometers)
Shoreline—131 miles (211 kilometers)
Greatest length (north to south)—180 miles (290 kilometers)
Greatest width (east to west)—93 miles (150 kilometers)
Geographic center—3 miles (4.8 kilometers) east of Ashland, at Belknap
Highest point—6,288 feet (1,917 meters), Mt. Washington
Lowest point—Sea level
Mean elevation—1,000 feet (305 meters)
Number of counties—10
Population—878,000 (1980 projection)
Rank in population—41st
Population density—79 persons per square mile (31 persons per square
       kilometer), 1970 census
Rank in density—20th
Population center—In Pembroke town, Merrimack County, 3.5 miles (5.6
       kilometers) east of Concord
Illiteracy rate—0.7 percent
Birthrate—14.6 per 1,000
Infant mortality rate—14.2 per 1,000 births
Physicians per 100,000—143

Principal cities—

| City | Population | |
|---|---|---|
| Manchester | 87,754 | (1970 census) |
| Nashua | 55,820 | |
| Concord | 30,022 | |
| Portsmouth | 25,717 | |
| Dover | 20,850 | |
| Keene | 20,467 | |
| Salem | 20,142 | |

## You Have a Date with History

1508—Giovanni de Verrazano sights White Mountains
1603—Martin Pring ventures up Piscataqua River
1605—Samuel de Champlain explores
1614—Captain John Smith investigates region
1623—First permanent European settlement, at Rye; Dover founded
1626—Portsmouth founded
1627—Chief Passaconaway establishes Penacook Confederacy
1629—John Mason names New Hampshire
1638—Exeter founded by the Reverend John Wheelwright; Hampton also founded
1642—First New England educational act; Darby Fields first to climb Mt. Washington; New Hampshire under government of Massachusetts
1659—Three Quakers hanged
1675—Durham suffers first attack of King Philip's War
1679—New Hampshire becomes crown colony
1689—Dover destroyed by French and Indian raid; New Hampshire rejoins Massachusetts briefly
1692—New Hampshire permanently separated from Massachusetts
1694—Durham sacked
1722—Captain Lovewell's War begins; Manchester settled
1727—Concord settled
1741—Boundary with Massachusetts settled
1756—First newspaper published in New Hampshire (oldest continuously published newspaper in United States)
1759—Indian troubles subsided
1761—First regular stagecoach run in America begins
1764—King establishes west bank of Connecticut River as New Hampshire-Vermont boundary
1771—Dartmouth College graduates first class
1774—Royal powder seized at Fort William and Mary
1775—Royal Governor, John Wentworth, flees New Hampshire
1776—New Hampshire approves first constitution of any of the colonies; later, votes for independence
1778—Thirty-five towns of New Hampshire attempt to join Independent Republic of Vermont
1788—New Hampshire becomes ninth and deciding state of Union
1805—*The Old Man of the Mountains* discovered
1808—Concord made permanent capital
1812—New Hampshire sends 35,000 men to War of 1812
1819—Dartmouth College Case argued and won by Daniel Webster
1832—Indian Stream Republic declared
1840—Webster-Ashburton Treaty finally establishes border with Canada

1849 — First New Hampshire railroad begins operation
1852 — New Hampshire-born Franklin Pierce becomes president
1861 — Civil War begins, in which 32,500 from New Hampshire serve; carriage
       road opens to top of Mt. Washington
1869 — Cog railroad opened to top of Mt. Washington
1872 — Nansen Ski Club founded at Berlin, said to be first in United States
1876 — Constitution revised to permit non-Protestant officials
1899 — First auto climbs to top of Mt. Washington
1905 — Treaty of Portsmouth signed
1917 — World War I begins, in which 20,000 from New Hampshire serve
1919 — Statewide public school system established
1923 — University of New Hampshire named officially
1934 — Supreme Court confirms west bank of Connecticut River as New
       Hampshire-Vermont boundary
1935 — Amoskeag Manufacturing Company of Manchester fails
1936 — Extensive floods
1941 — World War II begins, in which 60,000 from New Hampshire are in service
1959 — Scenic Kancamagus highway opened
1964 — New Hampshire revives system of lottery
1971 — Total value of goods produced reaches over $1 billion a year
1975 — New Hampshire loses territorial water boundary dispute
1976 — Wyman-Durkin election dispute won by Durkin
1979 — Hugh Gallen becomes governor

*Glen Ellis Falls at Pinkham Notch.*

## Thinkers, Doers, Fighters

*People of renown who have been associated with New Hampshire*

Adams, Isaac
Benet, Stephen Vincent
Cadman, Charles Wakefield
Cass, Lewis
Chase, Salmon Portland
Cheney, Pierce
Chickering, Jonas
Churchill, Winston (novelist)
Clough, Enos
Copland, Aaron
Crawford, Ethan Allen
Dickson, John
Dix, John Adams
Downing, Lewis
Eddy, Mary Baker
Fortune, Amos
French, Daniel Chester
Frost, Robert
Gage, John H.
Greeley, Horace
Hawthorne, Nathaniel
Howe, Elias

Kilmer, Joyce
King, Thomas Starr
Kittredge, Walter
MacDowell, Edward
MacDowell, Marian Nevins
Marsh, Sylvester
Morrill, John
Orozco, Jose Clemente
Parrish, Maxfield
Passaconoway (Sagamore or Chief)
Pierce, Franklin
Robinson, Edwin Arlington
Saint-Gaudens, Augustus
Stark, John
Sullivan, John
Webster, Daniel
Wentworth, Benning
Wentworth, John
Wentworth, (Long) John
Wheelock, Eleazar
Whittier, John Greenleaf
Wilson, Henry

90

## Governors of New Hampshire (Since Statehood)

John Langdon 1788-1789
John Sullivan 1789-1790
Josiah Bartlett 1790-1794
John T. Gilman 1794-1805
John Langdon 1805-1809
Jeremiah Smith 1809-1810
John Langdon 1810-1812
William Plumer 1812-1813
John T. Gilman 1813-1816
William Plumer 1816-1819
Samuel Bell 1819-1823
Levi Woodbury 1823-1824
David L. Morrill 1824-1827
Benjamin Pierce 1827-1828
John Bell 1828-1829
Benjamin Pierce 1829-1830
Matthew Harvey 1830-1831
Samuel Dinsmoor 1831-1834
William Badger 1834-1836
Isaac Hill 1836-1839
John Page 1839-1842
Henry Hubbard 1842-1844
John Steele 1844-1846
Anthony Colby 1846-1847
Jared W. Williams 1847-1849
Samuel Dinsmoor, Jr. 1849-1852
Noah Martin 1852-1854
Nathaniel B. Baker 1854-1855
Ralph Metcalf 1855-1857
William Haile 1857-1859
Ichabod Goodwin 1859-1861
Nathaniel S. Berry 1861-1863
Joseph A. Gilmore 1863-1865
Frederick Smyth 1865-1867
Walter Harriman 1867-1869
Onslow Stearns 1869-1871
James A. Weston 1871-1872
Ezekiel A. Straw 1872-1874
James A. Weston 1874-1875
Person C. Cheyney 1875-1877

Benjamin F. Prescott 1877-1879
Natt Head 1879-1881
Charles H. Bell 1881-1883
Samuel W. Hale 1883-1885
Moody Currier 1885-1887
Charles H. Sawyer 1887-1889
David H. Goodell 1889-1891
Hiram A. Tuttle 1891-1893
John B. Smith 1893-1895
Charles A. Busiel 1895-1897
George A. Ramsdell 1897-1899
Frank W. Rollins 1899-1901
Chester B. Jordan 1901-1903
Nahum J. Batchelder 1903-1905
John McLane 1905-1907
Charles M. Floyd 1907-1909
Henry B. Quinby 1909-1911
Robert Bass 1911-1913
Samuel D. Felker 1913-1915
Rolland H. Spaulding 1915-1917
Henry W. Keyes 1917-1919
John H. Bartlett 1919-1921
Albert O. Brown 1921-1923
Fred H. Brown 1923-1925
John G. Winant 1925-1927
Huntley N. Spaulding 1927-1929
Charles W. Tobey 1929-1931
John G. Winant 1931-1935
H. Styles Bridges 1935-1937
Francis P. Murphy 1937-1941
Robert O. Blood 1941-1945
Charles M. Dale 1945-1949
Sherman Adams 1949-1953
Hugh Gregg 1953-1955
Lane Dwinell 1955-1959
Wesley Powell 1959-1963
John W. King 1963-1969
Walter R. Peterson, Jr. 1969-1973
Meldrim Thomson, Jr. 1973-1979
Hugh Gallen 1979-

# Index

93

94

## PICTURE CREDITS

## ABOUT THE AUTHOR

With the publication of his first book for school use when he was twenty, **Allan Carpenter** began a career as an author that has spanned more than 135 books. After teaching in the public schools of Des Moines, Mr. Carpenter began his career as an educational publisher at the age of twenty-one when he founded the magazine *Teachers Digest*. In the field of educational periodicals, he was responsible for many innovations. During his many years in publishing, he has perfected a highly organized approach to handling large volumes of factual material: after extensive traveling and having collected all possible materials, he systematically reviews and organizes everything. From his apartment high in Chicago's John Hancock Building, Allan recalls, "My collection and assimilation of materials on the states and countries began before the publication of my first book." Allan is the founder of Carpenter Publishing House and of Infordata International, Inc., publishers of *Issues in Education* and *Index to U. S. Government Periodicals*. When he is not writing or traveling, his principal avocation is music. He has been the principal bassist of many symphonies, and he managed the country's leading non-professional symphony for twenty-five years.